CULTURAL SILENCE
AND WOUNDED SOULS:

Black Men Speak About Mental Health

Edited by **Mark Tuggle**
Foreword by **Cleo Manago**

Design/Layout: Darlene A. Gist
Cover Photo: Jamel Shabazz

ISBN: 9798385875603

PUBLISHED AND PRINTED IN THE U.S.A.
MMXXIII

TABLE OF CONTENTS

ACKNOWLEDGEMENTS/THANK YOU

Cultural Silence and Wounded Souls: Black Men Speak about Mental Health

Thank you to my loving parents, Lawrence and Mary Tuggle.

Thank you to my spiritual advisor, Francisco Wing.

Thank you to my Copy Editor/Proofreader, Ayanna McNeill, for her integrity, passion and skill with cultivating a meaningful, purposeful and valuable anthology.

Thank you to Darlene Gist, the caring, prudent and resourceful graphics editor who graced me with the spirit of her discernment, enthusiasm and flexibility.

Thank you to everyone listed below for their love, support and wisdom:

David Brooks
Marissa Crespo, Esq.
Shawn Dove
Anthony Duncan
Gregory Gates
Darian Hall
Alphonso Henderson
Rei Horst
Detrel Howell
Brandon Johnson
Ivan Juzang
Andre Robert Lee
Brian Lewis
Kevin McGruder
Darius Miles
Lorraine Minor
Jill Nagle
Rod Riisbrook
Phil Roundtree
Dr. Randy "Dr. S." Sconiers
Jamel Shabazz
Charles Stephens
James Tuggle
Adrianne Walker
Dr. Joseph White
Brandon Alexander Williams
Renee Wright
Malik Yusef

Barrie Cline
Chuck D
Aleece Duke
Nereida Ferran-Hansard
Paul George
James Earl Hardy
G Herbo
Anthony Howell
Durrell K. Howell
Troy Johnson
Dr. Robin R. Laysears-Smith
Sheba Legend
Glenn E. Martin
Gerald McRath
David Miller
Arron Muller
Osadebo Omokaro
Darnell Robinson
Donny Scarborough
Martinez Sellers
Debra Sledge
Chris Thomas
Kevin Vaden
Farr Well
Emil Wilbekin
Andrew Woods
Yannick Yalipende
Alex Zucker

Cultural Silence and Wounded Souls:
Black Men Speak about Mental Health

In 2019, 547,543 individuals identified as Black and male were born in the US. Abruptly ushered from the warm, reliable comfort of the womb they discovered their breath, then lungs, making it possible to audibly express the sound (or vibration, if they were deaf) of their first introduction to trauma: to tears. Yet to have any idea of how familiar with these particular sensations they would become over their lifetime; and few spaces would be safe enough for them to tell anyone.

Amidst a glare of bright light the shock and novelty of human touch is sensed as a mob of giants huddle around to see if he is alive. He detects a familiar cadence which became faint at his brisk entry into this new world in the near distance. It was the first pulse he ever sensed back when he was a she - all human embryos physically begin as female. Moving closer and closer it brought relief and comfort with his mother's heartbeat as she held him tight as if he was precious, loved and valuable. Concurrently, this African descended neonatal inherited a society which contradicts the idea of him being precious, loved and valuable at every juncture.

With little to no guidance (unless he is very fortunate), he is now on the precarious path from being a Black baby boy. . .

- To a menace to society.
- To being a target, placed in conflict with his own humanity.
- To being told to act like a man with no clear or rational assistance on how to be a man.
- To devaluing his abilities to feel human, care for, and nurture others, especially another Black person.
- To statistically being the last hired and the first fired.
- To being called a nigga, even by other Black people, regardless of the fact racist whites invented the insult during the US Black enslavement period.
- To being 30% more likely to die from preventable heart disease.
- To being 60% more likely to die from a preventable stroke.

- To being 15 times more likely than white males to be killed unarmed by white police, white vigilantes, or other Black males who, ironically, inherit the same societal gauntlet.

. . .while he disproportionately represents the most intellectually capable and gifted children on record, excelling in almost every human category, including science, education, math, sports, literature, art, music, history, architecture, and even making love, so they say.

Many like him will never know of the greatness within their DNA footprint until they are too heartbroken or whitewashed to care. The recent congressional dismissal of Critical Race Theory (or Fact) helps to ensure this. Instead, soon after birth he will be inundated by myths of inferiority to a white Jesus, white dolls, Santa Claus and Superman, and being from a people whose most remarkable achievement was being freed from slavery by (so-called) benevolent white people. Intoxicated with illusions of inadequacy, confusion and the residue of emasculating and racist programming he may spend more time proving he is a man, or a woman, than learning how to be what he is: one of the greatest gifts to humanity.

Cultural Silence and Wounded Souls: Black Men Speak about Mental Health, edited by Mark J. Tuggle, seeks to intervene on the previously described voyage. With a seminal array of brilliant Black male narrators he guides readers toward healing insights, opportunities and the literacy necessary to stimulate awakening. Tuggle has granted us who dared to be born amid the maddening myths of white male supremacy and misandrynoir a powerful path to our recovery, nurturance, reflection and self-discovery.

Enjoy,
Cleo Manago

"There is a vaccine for the COVID 19 virus, but there is no vaccine for mental health. So as a nation, as community leaders, as public health leaders, we need to think about how we provide the support and the resources and create the spaces to help people deal with the trauma, the emotional, physical symptoms – anxiety, helplessness, nausea, headaches – that they may be struggling with."

– David R. Williams (How unjust police killings damage the mental health of Black Americans, 2018).

America has never been a safe place for a Black man to express his true feelings while living on stolen land. In fact, the desire for enslaved Africans to escape colonial plantations - which in some cities are now golf courses - was described as a mental illness, Drapetomania, by Samuel A. Cartwright, a physician who joined the Confederate States of America in the mid-1800s.

Cartwright said the slaves should be kept in a submissive state and treated like children with *"care, kindness, attention and humanity to prevent and cure them from running away."* If they became dissatisfied with their "condition" he felt they should be whipped as a prevention from running away. Cartwright further justified his racist theories by relying on Christian scripture.

The states are united in white male genealogy/generational patriarchy, power and privilege. As such, Black men endured centuries of brutality, domination, imperialism, lynching, murder, oppression, rape and violence. Anti-Black misandry, not baseball, is America's favorite pastime.

Dr. Tommy J. Curry says, *"Black males have been characterized as violent, misogynist, predatory rapists by gender theorists dating back to mid-nineteenth century ethnologists to contemporary intersectional feminists. These caricatures of Black men and boys are not rooted in any actual studies or empirical findings, but the stereotypes found throughout* various racist social scientific literatures that held Black males to be *effeminate while nonetheless hyper masculine and delinquent."* (Misandric Mischaracterizations of Black Males, 2018).

From the auction block to TikTok, Black Buck to Ed Buck, 1619 to COVID-19, the Middle Passage to a Rites of Passage, slave patrols to police brutality, George Washington to George Floyd, the Revolutionary War to the Revolution Will Not Be Televised, the Great Migration to Mass Incarceration, Black men, through grace and mercy, are still here, but . . .

What is a man?
Who can define true manhood?
When, if ever, did we become men in the US?
Where, if anywhere, can I go to learn about masculinity?
Why should I accept my father's views on gender expression?

Our hurt is deep.
Our pain is unique.
Our suffering is quiet.
Our trauma is violence.

I live with mental illness: anxiety and depression. I don't take medication. I was diagnosed in February 1995 at 34 years old, 125 pounds, homeless, jobless, penniless — and using drugs in the grips of self-destruction. My self-esteem was non-existent. I lacked confidence, resented authority and trusted no one. I was a bitter, miserable and unhappy individual.

Two months prior, in December 1994, I was diagnosed HIV-positive. I confided in a trusted friend, a Black lesbian with AIDS, who offered three life-altering suggestions: 1) find a holistic health practitioner; 2) join an HIV-positive support group; and 3) get into therapy.

I was cool with her first two suggestions, but therapy? Therapy? *"Isn't therapy for rich, crazy white people?"* I asked her. She laughed and said, *"I'm in therapy."* I was shocked but she assured me therapy was helpful to her spiritual journey of emotional healing. I was attracted to her spirit, believed in her transparency and decided to give it a try.

Our first session was on a weekday afternoon. I didn't know what to do or expect or say. My therapist was a 26 year-old heterosexual woman from Bosnia. She was friendly, pleasant and respectful upon greeting me. I sat down, uncomfortable and very nervous. I looked her in the eye and defiantly asked, *"What are you going to do for me?"*

She paused and then responded, *"I am here to assist you with the quality of your life."*

Damn. I was fucked up. I know now fucked up is not a feeling but I was feeling fucked up. I didn't believe my life could be worthy of quality. I was confused yet excited. My face wore the complexion of perplexion. This woman seemed genuine. My default personality is cynical, guarded and suspicious. Yet oddly enough I was hopeful: which also left me terrified.

I don't remember anything else about our first session. But I was committed to seeing where the unknown might lead me in weekly unscripted one-on-one dialogue with a stranger. We rarely spoke about HIV. To my surprise and delight she modeled compassion, empathy and understanding. My therapist engaged the little boy inside of me who felt abandoned, betrayed, disappointed, invisible, misunderstood, rejected, sad and unappreciated.

We met regularly for three consecutive years. One of our sessions was in Central Park on a beautiful summer day. During another session we met inside an organic food store where she encouraged me to eat healthier meals, read food labels and take prudent risks. She once asked would I consider being "under hypnosis." Initially, the idea frightened me yet I went forward and benefited emotionally from the unconventional experience.

Our sessions began to unearth my self-imposed prisons of guilt, remorse and unforgiveness. I looked forward to speaking my truth in a private space. Yet I was uncomfortable examining aspects of my past which haunted me for years: the physical, sexual and verbal abuse I endured were secrets destined for my unmarked grave.

My image of being assured, cool and invincible masked brokenness, shame and terror. I lacked coping skills in my relationships with others. I avoided conflict, feared intimacy and lived recklessly. I believed I had no choice and no voice when difficulties arose. I distanced people when they disagreed with me. I harbored resentments when I couldn't get my way. I viewed the world as cruel, hostile and unsafe. I was arrogant when someone pointed out a mistake.

Therapy helped me look inward for the source of my discontent. I learned to stop blaming others for my feelings, issues and shortcomings. We discussed boundaries, goals and plans. I learned to celebrate small victories and treat myself kindly. I learned to be assertive with difficult people in unpleasant situations. I learned to say no and not feel guilty.

I was dismayed when my therapist chose another path in her career. She offered a few recommendations for other therapists at the same clinic but I declined. I partnered with three male (Black and Brown) therapists, on and off for about seven years, until I felt empowered to let go and move on with faith, humility and trust. Self-love is self-care!

I stopped using drugs on May 20, 1995. Today, I stay clean living by spiritual principles and serving humanity one day at a time. Today, I pray daily and meditate regularly. I have used acupuncture, colonics and yoga to help me feel whole. I met same gender-loving (SGL) men of African descent in New York City – like myself - who taught me to embody critical thinking, cultural affirmation and self-determination in my daily affairs.

Therapy is not a one-size-fits-all solution. At 61, I'm still a work in progress and feel good about myself; on most days. When disturbing thoughts and/or painful emotions come I don't harm myself. I attend support groups, exercise in a gym or park, journal my feelings, listen to music, speak with a trusted friend, take a power nap or watch comedy, movies and sports.

As a modality, institution and practice, therapy offers a relatively new paradigm shift for Black men. Yet, Black men do have a cultural relationship with therapeutic conversations. We chop it up at/in barbershops, car pools, front porches, holiday parties, kitchen tables, locker rooms, neighborhood cookouts, park benches, spiritual gatherings and wedding ceremonies to foster brotherhood, friendship and intimacy.

In Rwanda, some cultural practices for healing depression include basking in the sun, dance, drumming and engaging community. Black Americans can benefit from natural and/or everyday "therapy" practices such as being around water, breathing in and out, cooking, gardening, humor, jogging, painting, playing with kids, spending time with nature, rest and singing.

God turned my private pain into public purpose. The shameful silent stigma of living with mental health issues is a poignant reality (and remains taboo for many Black men) in 2022. According to the Black Emotional and Mental Health Collective (BEAM), mental health is a person's relationship to the state of their psychological and emotional being.

A number of prominent Black men, in the spirit of honesty, transparency and vulnerability, have publicly admitted challenges with mental health. Wayne Brady, Kid Cudi, DeMar DeRozan, Andrew Gillum, G Herbo, Dwayne Johnson, Brandon Marshall, Vic Mensa, Trevor Noah,

Big Sean, Royce White and Metta World Peace – bravely remind us all, sometimes:

"It's okay to not be okay." – Solomon Thomas, defensive lineman, New York Jets.

Each contributor in this intergenerational anthology has a unique cultural perspective on this provocative subject matter. These brothers are beautiful, bold and brilliant. Also, they come from diverse backgrounds: advocates, businessmen, clinicians, educators, filmmakers, lawyers, musicians, poets and scholars, etc.

Additionally, the anthology lends a number of important resources for people. There are books to read, helplines to call, organizations to utilize, podcasts to watch, service providers to engage and websites to visit. My intention is to serve as a conduit of healing, restoration and success for Black men – and their allies. **If the collective consciousness of this content prevents one Black male suicide our pain will not be in vain!**

In Loving Service,
Mark Tuggle

DESPONDENCE
by David Malebranche

I imagine this is what death feels like.

Not a solitary moment of pain or exquisite agony followed by a rapid descent into permanent darkness, but a blurring of days so time and space have no defined compartments and each just blends into the next with ease and disregard. A perpetual state of paralytic inertia, where you feel like you should be doing something, but cannot.

Feeling like something should or could be different, but you can't quite embrace what it is. An existence where one churns through mundane activities out of habit, treading water before sinking to the murky depths below.

It could be a heaviness more than discomfort, like a million different raindrops hitting your skin at the same time – each one with a sharpened tip to penetrate the flesh, burying deep within skin, muscle, and bones. Density becomes so inevitable that the ground caves beneath you, swallowing you whole.

You struggle to remain upright, but the rain is relentless – not a light mist you could easily endure or an abundant downpour from which you could run and seek shelter. No, this shower is a steady, persistent assault from above, one that melts bodies like piles of sand on concrete. At first you become mushy, then mud-like in consistency until swept away in diluted puddles that flow like rivers.

It doesn't feel like how it's portrayed in the movies. A white women with wispy hair, sitting in the corner of the room like a static figurine, flicking a light switch on and off while symmetrical tears stream down the center of her alabaster cheeks. She gathers herself after a couple of days and visits a therapist in a posh downtown building where she is greeted by a smiling receptionist, bowls of candy at the front desk, and the soothing white noise of an aquarium.

Her equally white therapist listens intently to her musings, nods at appropriate times, and mutters neutral utterances between reflexive "how does that make you feel" inquiries. A magical "a-ha" breakthrough moment occurs after a few weeks, and now there is a new lease on life – an opportunity to go back to normal. If that doesn't happen, there's always medication to tinker with neurotransmitters; when things aren't actually better, redacted brain chemistry will make her believe so.

For Black folks it doesn't fit neatly into a medical textbook definition of criteria based on countless studies with thousands of Europeans. It exists as anger, the Trojan horse of sorrow and despair, a product of an odd concoction of battling internalized masculine tropes with secretive longing for connections to more traditionally feminine feelings.

For Black folks it's choosing isolation over connection. Blunting feelings over allowing them to wash over. Cursing somebody the fuck out instead of telling them how sad you are and how much you need them now more than ever before. It's saying "I'm okay" when you're really not.

For Black folks it's about going to work regardless of how we feel. We endure not finding a therapist who looks like us even if we are fortunate enough to have the insurance or financial ability to pay for it.

For Black folks it's a cramped waiting area in a dilapidated building. Nasty attitudes from receptionists and moldy walls. A counselor who is overworked, underpaid, and seems disinterested in our well-being. A knee-jerk prescription instead of delving into the work of exploring our deeply rooted causes.

It manifests as compensatory behavior with tragic self-destructive consequences.

Smoke it away.
Drink it away.
Shop it away.
Gamble it away.
Sleep it away.
Eat it away.
Sex it away.

I've tried most, if not all of these things in the past. I choose to experience it differently today. I choose to banish myself to a self-imposed purgatory for the immediate future. I don't want to hear "you'll be fine" or "you'll get through this" from well-intentioned friends and colleagues.

I don't want to go to work and resume exhausting normality as if there is nothing wrong. This is part of my journey and I want to feel it.

I want to sit with it as if it were an unwanted guest and I were being forced to entertain it. I want to feel the ache instead of running away in fear. I want to face it, invite it in, and let it seep through me. I want to be absorbed into my pores and change the fabric of my being so I don't fully recognize the person I was before and can't quite make out the person I will become. I should be present for what it is and who I am now.

I miss the Black man I once was. Grief changed him. The man sitting in his place is broken and bruised like an aged prizefighter at the end of a heavyweight bout. His eyes are swollen shut and delirious with blood and crusted debris. It's hard to imagine "it gets better" when I can't conceptualize when or how it will. All I see is vast space with uncertain beginnings and ends. I want to get closer so I can visualize it clearly, but I can't adjust my eyes to the polluted glare.

All I know is I miss my Dad.

I miss his smile. I miss his voice and booming laugh. I miss how he showed me what a proud Black man was without having to say a word. I miss his corny jokes and the stories he told a thousand times for multitudes of people. I miss calling on his infinite guidance and wisdom. I miss him challenging me and pissing me off to the point where I once foolishly wished he was dead. I miss the life I knew when he was physically here. I miss how home was not a building, but an atmosphere he created with his own two hands.

It's been less than a year.

I miss my Dad.

This feels like death to me.

A TRIGGERED LIFE

by Keith Mascoll

The secret you kept the longest is the hardest to admit.
I just did not want to face it.
It.
I was forced to deal with it
Because I moved back to my childhood home.
Stepping into the front door.
Hit me like a lightning bolt,
and jolted me with every abusive sensation that happened years ago.
I sat with my wife by the front
door and just told her what I could tell her.
I mean how do you even talk about it?
How do I make her understand
why I only talked about her abusing me and not him?

I try.
I try to face it.
Everyday.
I try to get rid of it with
my power.
My intellect.
The wisdom my mother gave me.
But secrets have a way of creating
Its own climate and conditions.

Rain.
Storms.
Fog.

I believe it could all go away.
I believe if I close my eyes
it would all go away by morning.
I've gotta believe it.

I've gotta believe there is
A River Jordan for me.
A place to lay my burden down.

Everyday.
Everyday...
I get tired of facing it.
But I'm only one step away
from the shadow.
I call it 'the shadow' because
it takes light from me.
Changes my weather.
Changes me.

I believe it could all go away.
I believe if I close my eyes
it would all go away by morning.
I've gotta believe it.
I've gotta believe it.

I'm one step ahead but everyday
is different.
Sometimes I don't have the
energy to keep running.
I know I'm not supposed to
run but that's what I do.
A man is not supposed to have
this problem so why not run away from it?

I get consumed by the shadow.
I get consumed to the point
where everything shuts down.
Then.
What I really feel.
To be real.
I feel like my manhood disappears.

A MESSAGE TO ISOLATED BLACK MEN

by T. Hasan Johnson, Ph.D.

"Let me tell you something. A man ain't a goddamn ax. Chopping, hacking, busting every goddamn minute of the day. Things get to him. Things he can't chop down because they're inside."

— Toni Morrison, Beloved

"You may be deceived if you trust too much, but you will live in torment if you don't trust enough."

— Frank Crane

Black men have been conditioned to believe we should not feel pain, and to acknowledge it is somehow a display of weakness. Although manhood in the West has been subject to this paradigm, all men have not been imagined as hyper-masculine, violent, and hyper-sexual threats to order and civilization like Black men.

Put another way, Black men have never been allowed to be men, but have been simultaneously used as an unrealistic standard of both a visceral and yet dangerous masculinity. This idea of Black manhood has meant (even) Black male children are viewed as older than they are while – consequently – men are considered unworthy of emotional support. Black men and women have been trained to see Black men in such ways and men suffer because of it.

The rates of suicide for Black, isolated men are too high. Remember it is okay to reach out and accept companionship and support from whomever you trust it from (although this might require some opening up on your part).

When Black men feel isolated and unsupported, it can be difficult to find help because people often do not know how to support you. In film and television, women (even Black women) have "methods" for helping one another which are known and celebrated: clubbing, discussion circles, shopping, etc. Even children are shown in media being cheered up by loving adults, but with men people are stumped.

This can be even worse during the holidays, when social expectation demand men make others' holidays, special – often requiring financial sacrifices we may not be able to make. Of course, most people struggle during the holidays with this, but for Black men, social expectation increases this stress: children and women have been conditioned to expect men to provide while showing Black men they are not needed, and they can enjoy life without them.

When attempting to support Black men, some will even become hostile to you in an effort to "toughen" you up, while others will back away and isolate you even more trying to "give you space." Others will give you advice and tell you everything you did wrong in an attempt to help, but are oblivious to how much critique hurts when you are depressed.

Few realize how presence is just as important to Black men as anyone else. Simply providing support by giving attention is incredibly reaffirming. Recognizing a man beyond his utility reaffirms his humanity, as does acknowledging the limitations of our cultural training in regards to Black male roles in our cultural milieu.

Furthermore, the isolation is often both conditional and self-imposed. People are taught to fear you, and the dynamic we're bred with to compete with one another as young Black men keeps us from building relationships in life – particularly over the age of 35. I implore you to find the drive to reach out, especially to the youth, and create ways to show them what you've learned in life. This will both enliven you and help them.

The killings of Black males by police, vigilantes, and other Black males, has been constant, but must be challenged. Find ways to suit your spirit and temperament to challenge this; whether in an organization, in protest demonstrations, in writing, or anything else. Just choose something to reach the public and not just something in your head.

Finally, no matter how bad it gets (especially during the holiday season), remember what hip hop legend KRS-ONE once said, "Stay alive and all things'll change around." Have faith, if nothing else, in this reality: the only constant is change, and this includes for the better. Whether you believe in meditation or the Divine (God), engage your source more often. There is no limit on how often you may do this. It is your birthright. Let it fuel you.

MY STORY
by Charles Crouch

I was 26 years old when I finally stopped playing, literally, with "death," and decided to swallow every inch of pride I had and check myself into a mental institution. I probably hadn't eaten a solid meal in days. I had no strength left. When I had to use the bathroom, I would often crawl. I hadn't showered in days. I was calling out from work for days on end.

Phone calls went unanswered. I didn't want to deal with anyone. It comes to a point where you get tired of people asking you what is wrong and don't quite know how to answer. When you say, "I don't know," you mean just that. It's an honest answer.

Everything was a complete blur.

I called the only person I could really trust – my mother. She came over, picked me up and took me to the hospital. I distinctly remember talking to the nurse as they processed me in. It was almost as if I was going to jail in a sense. They take things away from you they feel you may harm yourself with. You are given a number for privacy purposes. Anyone who calls has to have this secret number.

There was a moment I will never forget. A clearly overworked nurse got frustrated with me because my arm kept shaking while she was trying to draw my blood. It was embarrassing. Here I was, feeling as if I was on the brink of dying, and a nurse is mad with me because I am messing up her "morning rounds" routine. I stayed there five days. Some family members came to visit; my parents, siblings, and the young lady I was dating at the time came every single day.

Life has been different for me ever since I checked out that memorable day 18 years ago. After being clinically diagnosed with severe major depression and anxiety I move differently, not physically, but mentally. I have been on several different medications. You have to figure out which one works for you. It took me awhile.

Living with depression is one thing. Being a Black man with clinically diagnosed depression is a completely different monster. I have often said the majority of, if not all, Black men suffer from a sort of societal Post Traumatic Stress Disorder (PTSD). We deal with triggers, and anxiety which non-Black and Brown people rarely experience.

These issues range from police encounters, a white supremacist society, financial disparities between Black men and white men, etc. We deal with these things daily. When a police vehicle gets behind me I have a full panic attack. And, I am a fully insured, licensed and legal driver.

It's an unconventional way to live, but necessary for someone with my condition. However, if you encounter mood swings, high anxiety, extreme lows, unexplainable sadness, and chemical imbalances in the brain you have no control over, it can make for a flustered existence.

Do I still have bad days? Yes. I still have bad weeks for that matter. The key to overcoming these days is utilizing coping mechanisms, and constantly reminding myself I've endured this before. Every episode of depression feels like the first time. Depression is not something you can "positive thought," away. Depression is not something you can simply "shake off."

Depression is literally not being capable of thinking a positive thought. Every scenario has a bad ending. You are literally "super glued," to every mistake you have made in life and "that" is why you are in the position you are currently in. A common misconception for most people who do not live with depression: people are simply "having a bad day."

It is the equivalent of comparing a common cold to lung cancer.

And, it's unfair. You are literally dealing with something you have little control over. You can only treat it the best way you know how until it passes. At times it passes quickly; sometimes it does not. Most times I HAVE to power through. I have a son to take care of, bills to pay, and a life to try and live as fulfilling as possible for him.

I will say I am blessed. They key to overcoming episodes of depression is to have a wonderful support system. I have family and friends who recognize when they have not heard from me in a few days. They see my social media has been quiet for a while. I haven't texted or called. I'm not sending them a goofy meme, or telling a funny story in my journey of fatherhood.

This is unlike me. I'm generally a silly and goofy dude. They recognize a break in patterns. This is imperative in recognizing depressive episodes.

Your tone is different on phone calls. Answers are short when talking – and that's even if you feel like talking.

Unfortunately, many brothers don't have this luxury. Black men are surrounded by people who may call them "weak," or people who constantly tell them to "man up." Their beliefs are even worse when that person is your spouse. You have to have someone who understands the disease of depression, and not someone who just sees the visual representation of depression. The visual alone can be very deceiving.

I recall when I was married I often felt my ex-wife did not fully understand my depression. It's almost as if while we were dating she was more in tune with me. Possibly, once we became married she may have felt as if I needed to "suck it up," and be a husband. There were times I did not feel comfortable confiding in her. I had a fear of being reprimanded or subliminally ridiculed. A man needs his significant other to be in his safe space. He should be able to be completely vulnerable around her.

Marriage is probably THE ONLY place he will have that type of expose'. There were times after we separated and ultimately divorced she would use my illness against me. She used it to ridicule me; asking if I had taken my meds, or what was wrong with my brain, knowing it was a particularly stressful and hurtful time for me. It was bad, and it took me several years to recover from that period. Honestly, the recovery is ongoing.

Living with depression, ironically, can be positive. You develop empathy through your personal struggles. When I look at other people I am not so quick to pass judgment on them. You recognize they may be hurting and reacting from sheer ignorance of a deeper issue yet to be discovered when themselves. Due to learned warning signals as a result of personal experience and also educating myself I see traits in other brothers I know may be dealing with depression.

In my relationships, whether they are family members or close friends, a spirit of compassion is developed. Once you truly understand and live with depression, you do not want anybody you love to deal with it – and definitely not deal with it alone. I believe a person who has truly dealt with any type of pain can help someone else who deals with that same type of pain.

My son, Jordan, is the absolute love of my life. At the tender age of eight years old, I am very keen to his emotional state. I never deny him the opportunity to express how he is feeling, no matter how miniscule it may seem to me as an adult. Studies have shown depression can be genetic. I make sure Jordan understands he can always talk to me.

I have instilled the value of two-way communication in him since birth. I pray my son will not be diagnosed with depression later in life seeing he already has the target of black skin covering him. I look for those warning signs early. I want him to have a fruitful life and a healthy support system if needed.

Living with depression is not easy. You are one trigger or negative thought away from having the best day of your life to feeling like your entire world is engulfed in flame and your very sanity is the gasoline. However, hope and the will to keep living is just as powerful. Do I take meds to maintain chemical and emotional balance? Yes. Am I ashamed of that anymore? No.

We all need help in various forms. I take medicine, pray to a Higher Power, reach out to loved ones when I need to, and go to therapy when I need an educated ear. I remain confident my struggle is not for me, but for somebody who may need my support, love, listening ear, shoulder to cry on, advice, and presence when they deal with the same thing.

It's not the way some folx describe it: selfish. Cowardly. Unimaginable. Short-sighted. As someone who has, several times, survived ideations in the abyss of my greatest emotional pain; someone who survived a suicide attempt as a 16 years-old. But as "crazy" or uncomfortable as it may sound to folx who've never experienced the depth of my despair, suicide is a deeply profound act of self-love...

There, I said it!

Any person's attempted suicide experience is real for me because on Sunday, April 12, 2020 past harmful thoughts revisited my soul. I was triggered by the seeming departure of a man I considered my greatest love amidst this global pandemic which denies the aching comfort of affectionate hugs. As such, ending my life seemed the most protective thing to do.

This pain, for anyone who experiences it, seems deceptive yet offers clear tunnel vision: little exists between the pain of that moment and the courage to end that moment. No doubt, loved ones are quick to lament "so much to live for exists." Still, all rebuttals are betrayed in that moment. In 2006, my friend Ricky Williams ended his life by jumping off the Golden Gate Bridge. I was haunted by the informing call not because I couldn't understand why – I do understand why. Ricky said, "I'm tired, I'm tired. Those of you that I love know who you are. May God bless you."

My late friend's words, similar to Phyllis Hyman's suicide note, carry an all-too familiar surrender. I, too, was born July 6: a hyper-emotional Cancerian, moving through life wherever the light of love seemed to land. I remember the day Hyman left our planet like it was yesterday. Her beautiful, emotional and gifted voice seems familiar to me. She offers a kind of longing, for any empath, was so painful because it marks what philosopher Lyotard might call a wail that substitutes a phrase. Sometimes folx have no words for their unique life experiences, but they sing loud and clear. Her suicide note exclaims, "I'm tired," and her surrender resonates for me in the way it speaks to a resilience which falls short of the salvation needed to extend it.

Phyllis Hyman knew who she loved and likely who loved her. Did she win by ending her pain in that moment? Folx who lack her lived experience sometimes (by default) remark, "I'm still here." But not everyone can mercifully survive the unbearable, uncomfortable and unspeakable pain she went through.

Many folx assume loved ones who commit suicide harbored mental health issues, lack of faith, betrayed Jesus, or the devil made them do it. Some folx believe the purchase of a rope, a communion of pills as salvation, or a loaded gun as a panacea are unfathomable. But I believe these so-called "weak acts," are, in fact, brave acts. Understanding my courage and forgiving myself during such powerful moments has always been my wake up call: "It hurts." "I can't live like this." "I can't live without him."

I gave my heart permission to sing these suicide notes at the pep rally before the event. Every July 6th I wear a t-shirt of either Hyman or Frieda Kahlo: we all share the same birthdate. Hyman died by suicide a week before her birthday. Kahlo's suicidal death was by pulmonary embolism a week after. One might say they both died from heartbreak. When I hear Phyllis sing, "Living All Alone," or I view Kahlo's plethora of poignant artwork, they both represent people who live for love, who empty everything for it, and feel empty without it.

My suicide attempt in high school was triggered by heartbreak. Even at 16, feeling betrayed by a God who didn't remove a same-sex love led to my effort to end the perpetual aching for the desire my religion would deny me. Upon later reflection my suicidal feelings were always fueled by love: a "this one will be the last one," love, or as Phyllis wailed a "when I give my love (this time)" love.

When I feel suicidal, I feel like an innocent boy cursed for my queer desire and remind myself often the world considers it a perversion. When I unearth the courage to love again, it feels like a fight in the face of everyone who ever told me queer love is wrong. Being in-love for many queer folx is an existential battle for affirmation most hetero folx take for granted.

As long as my love is affirmed there's every reason to live – yet when it seems to go away, life can seem meaningless. It's twisted logic of people like me who fall too hard, too fast. We flaunt the rationale of therapists or loved ones disturbed by their inefficiency and who often tell me "there is so much to live for." But for those who dare to end their lives, there isn't much to live for. Perhaps the healing desired can start with this crude reality.

The original title of my first book was Suicide Journal. The publication was a critical touchpoint in "Red Dirt Revival: a poetic memoir in

6 breaths" because it summarizes the painful truth of those who complete their courageous and self-loving final act. I always wanted to write this for those who had fallen but didn't. There's an ironic shaming of those who complete suicide in their death. As someone whose life work has involved suicide prevention, especially among LGBTQ+ teens, it's important to reveal how "senseless" suicide is to those who never considered it, yet how much sense it makes to its victims.

Rather than trying to make sense of suicide we could all do better to create a world where triggers fail, where hope is bountiful on the edge of despair, and where it's okay for people to not be okay. People who are suicidal don't need to be fixed: we need our pain affirmed. Life sucks. This hurts. It's unfair. Why? Because sometimes it just is. Against the tide of the dismissive "tomorrow will be better," "just get over it," or, "it gets better," we might humbly own we can't understand what we can't understand. The better question might be: "what do you need to be okay?" And, being prepared to ask "what else?"

On April 12, 2020 I needed to believe he loved me, even if he no longer wanted us to be partners. My reason for living would be measured by whether or not he called to say goodnight, like he did nearly every night we'd been together. My plea earlier that day I was "in a pretty bad space" was rejected as serious, evidenced by him not calling. My beloved is not a cruel man, he was simply managing his own pain and perhaps my perception of neglect in the moment created an opportunity to finally accept a spiritual truth about myself. I live for love. It's who I am, AND, that's okay, as it was for Phyllis, too.

"Where have you been all my life?
I was nothing, I was no one
Til' you came and made it right
Thought I didn't stand a chance
Til' I found this sweet romance
The answer boy, is you..."

Yeah, yeah, I know, I know. If you don't love yourself, how the hell are you gonna love anyone else? Saith RuPaul. Folx like me who live for love bear the empathic gift of seeing our best through our capacity to give love to another. The self-love rhetoric pitifully and certainly fails our counter-narrative. What I have needed to believe in these moments is there's still a chance, if not to love and be loved by the one I'm with, then surely by another love someday. This is the only (!) way I survived the projection of my own death – a death I know would surely hurt many, for all the ways I have seen salvation in it.

My friend Ricky said, "I'm tired. I'm tired."

Every time suicide enters the realm of possibility for me, I'm never quite sure what distracts it. I have always been grateful I survived, and perhaps that's just it. The "it gets better" is only convincing testimony I myself bear. Each time I've fallen in love, it's sweeter than the last. This hope is a dare against a dare. This hope is a salvation from salvation I think I understood back in 1999 when I wrote Suicide Journal with a pencil nub in psych unit:

I want to create a suicide journal, before the event, that I can read and be afraid of the consequences, and not follow through. I want suicide notes that sing soprano and baritone at one – meshing into the praise song my belly wails when it rumbles. There in the gut, where I beg for more strength to put up with what lies outside of this hospital window, I want to solicit an army of writing rebels...whose optimism and hope for heaven on earth is as sensible as a suicide journal: volatile, full of passion, wishing to be found before the exit, a daily manifest for salvation."

SAVING THE SOULS OF BLACK MEN: OPTIMAL MENTAL HEALTH AND WELL-BEING!
by Richard Rowe

"If you are silent about your pain, they'll kill you
and say you enjoyed it."

– Zora Neale Hurston

Mental health is a taboo subject for Black men. There is a general stigma associated with mental problems and illnesses. Various issues related to culture, masculinity and the socio-political environment often hinder Black men and young men from addressing problems related to mental health. Poverty, racism, and the impact of past trauma (particularly violence) are the primary contributing factors to the mental health disorders of Black men and young men.

I was a planner of and participant in a unique healing convening for Black men and young men, which was a special moment in time and space. Forum presenters with backgrounds in clinical psychology, family therapy, mental health counseling and transformational healing techniques delivered life-affirming and life-saving healing messages to the community of Black men and young men present. It was a critical and safe place where Black men could reflect, process some of their feelings and learn how to best address or enhance their mental health and well-being.

The men realized they are not weak to acknowledge fears providing for their families, or anxieties existing in a world in which Black men are devalued and their soul is trampled on each day. It was clear from the conversation Black men can work through their fears and worries by talking with other men - fathers, friends, siblings, therapists, or soon to be new friends in group therapy or other supportive spaces. These are spaces for us to heal. Although they require a bit of risk exposing one's emotional vulnerabilities, it is worth it; on the other side of risk is less anxiety, less depression, less stress and potential for self-harm and harm to their loved ones.

There was a call from the men present, and from many other Black men in the city, for more sessions and more healing opportunities for Black men, and young men. The Black Mental Health Alliance (BMHA) is giving serious consideration to what might/should come next to invest in and support safe spaces which allow Black men and young men to address, open up, and unpack the influences of historical/contemporary race-based trauma, toxic stress, chronic depression, thoughts of hyper-masculinity, and overwhelming exposure to violence which negatively affects their mental health and psychological well-being.

Here are some of the voices shared by the participants in the Souls of Black Men convening about their mental health – uncensored and unscripted.

Their heartfelt voices are honest, and, at times, unsettling. More important, these unified voices are courageous and strong. Their views point to deep rooted, and systemic issues underlying the mental health problems faced by Black men and young men. These problems are related to the social environment, the availability of services, and the way treatment currently offered can no longer be ignored.

"We are not supposed to seek help for our mental illness.

"In this society many of us feel alone. Who can we turn to?"

"Who really gives a damn about the Black man in America?"

"Racism has forced a lot of Black men to sit on top of their pain. They feel there are very few outlets to share their feelings of frustration with the system."

"Many of us have developed a what difference does it make attitude."

"After they told me, in their way, I had a mental disorder (after one session) and after only one conversation, I never went back. They did not care and neither did I."

"We are responsible for our mental health, but we need help and support."

"No Black man in America is ever mentally healthy."

"In this society the Black man feels he can never rest, he can never relax, or just be himself."

"If they do not try to understand you and step into your shoes, they can never get the diagnosis right. I really felt rejected and unworthy of help and support."

"Racism has caused many of us to believe we do not count, and our needs are not important."

"Even when we do everything right and play by all the rules, we still do not get the respect we deserve, and that is very, very stressful."

"This society only values what you do not who you are."

"How would you feel if you thought everyone around you was afraid of you, or thought you were getting ready to do something illegal?"

"There is still a lot of stereotyping of Black men in all the medical professions."

"We have a problem asking for help, especially from folks who we think we are the reasons for our mental illness."

These observations validate acute, debilitating feelings of nihilism, defined by Dr. Cornel West as the lived experience of coping with a life of horrifying meaninglessness, hopelessness, and (most important) "love-lessness." The frightening result is a numbing detachment from others and a self-destructive disposition toward the world. Life without meaning, hope, and love breeds a coldhearted, mean-spirited outlook which destroys the individual and others.

Listening to Black men and young men it was clear they wanted to change inside but find it difficult unless things on the outside changed as well. Sadly, "who can we turn to?" is still an existential challenge for many Black men, and they will continue to suffer in silence until they recognize the emotional and psychic pain they endure over time has led to an indescribable, unconscionable and irrefutable pain, suffering - and feelings of what Dr. Martin Luther King described as "no body ness." Their hurt points to the deep rooted, systemic issues underlying the mental health problems they face. Problems related to the social environment, to the availability of services, and the way treatment is offered can no longer be ignored.

What is the path toward healing and treatment for Black men today?

- Early intervention is critical. Outreach must be tailored specifically for Black men and health education must be delivered by trusted messengers.
- There must be greater support for mental health promotion and intervention initiatives specifically geared to Black males.
- Early intervention strategies must be developed for Black men and boys who are vulnerable to environmental and psychosocial factors which predispose them to self-destructive behaviors.
- Additional male support groups and healing circles are needed to help men with the healing process.
- There needs to be a culturally competent media education and awareness campaign about mental health and well-being specifically for Black men.
- We need a database of Black mental health professionals who understand the plight of Black men in this country

and who will not prejudge, but who will listen to their pain and feelings of frustration.

We need Community and Provider Service Delivery Systems to

- Conduct stigma awareness trainings at faith-based institutions, community-based organizations, and primary care settings.
- Educate providers on the identification, diagnosis and treatment of mental health issues for Black men and boys.
- Support academic-community partnerships to prioritize culturally competent academic health training and the delivery of health services.
- Improve referral and follow up mechanisms from the criminal justice system to community-based organizations, mental health facilities and substance abuse treatment systems.
- Assist in the creation of formal and informal systems to provide Black men opportunities to congregate and discuss problems they feel they cannot mention to most people.
- Encourage Black institutions, community leaders and health professionals to promote involvement and promotion of Black men in traditional and non-traditional institutional structures, groups and relationships (churches, family activities, fraternities, health retreats, group therapy, i.e.) within the Black community to offer cooperative and self-help approaches to stressful situations.

Finally, it was clear from the convening Black men can no longer be silent about their pain and the physiological and psychological toll which has been and remains life-threatening, group threatening and overwhelming, because:

- We are killing ourselves and each other.
- We are abusing our women.
- We are neglecting/abandoning our children.
- We are missing in action and we are missing from our families and communities.
- We are unable to receive love because we have forgotten how to love ourselves.
- Many of us are on a collision course and have forgotten life-sustaining, life-giving and life-affirming rituals, practices... our way.
- We are least likely to have an annual physical check-up.
- We are least likely to seek or ask for help for health-related illnesses.
- We are least likely to seek counseling, or therapeutic treatment for:

Depression
Stress
Anxiety
Bipolar Disorder
Ever present anger
Other behavioral disorders

The mental health and well-being of Black men, young men, and boys must become a moral imperative.

I am happy to be of service.

MACHISMO DOESN'T MAKE LATINX MEN STRONGER OR BETTER, TIME FOR SOMETHING NEW

by Jason Rosario

After witnessing one of the many moments when my stepfather was beating on my mother, I decided to stand up for my Mom and for us. Shit, if she was not going to fight back, I would. After all, I was becoming *el hombre de la casa:* the man of the house. I was working and helping to pay the bills, so handling my stepfather felt like one of my responsibilities, too.

I pushed him out of the door and on his way out he screamed, *"Si tu eres un hombre, baja conmigo!"* If I was a man, he said, come down with him. He challenged me to a fight.

Down in the lobby of my building, I watched him as he unbuttoned his shirt and rolled up his sleeves, egging me on to come out and fight with him in the January snow. I saw anger and pain in his eyes.

I don't know what stopped me from engaging him. I was already taller than most at 14, and I was confident I could have held my own. What I believe kept me from losing myself that night is the same thing which has inspired my growth as a man today. I now realize *machismo,* like any facet of patriarchy, destroys boys and men.

Machismo is a term used within Latinx communities, which describes an exaggerated expression of masculinity. It's a consequence of patriarchy which reinforces male dominance over women and femme people – a dominance which renders them dependent on men for all of their needs. Men are socialized to rule, fight, control, and win. In Latinx communities, these ideas, which render men as the dominant figure in and out of the home, is accepted by many.

It shouldn't be.

Machismo in Latinx culture allows for an all-out assault on the emotional, gender and sexual expressions of men. If one displays too much emotion, he must be a *pendejo* (e.g. punk). If he exhibits a good knack with the ladies, *que bacano!* (the man!); if the opposite is true, he is labeled a *maricon* (faggot). To survive, we are forced to adapt and conform, or risk acceptance by our peers and families. Trust me, I know.

I grew up between Washington Heights and the Bronx, New York. My upbringing wasn't unlike that of many other kids in my neighborhood. Many of us were raised by single mothers who worked long shifts to make sure we had enough *plantanos* to go with that Chef Boyardee.

In some cases, whether by necessity or convenience, we also filled the role of *de facto* husbands, fathers, and confidants. In all cases, many of us were encouraged to act as if we were men while we were boys. We were forced to mature before we had any understanding of manhood.

I learned how to perform masculinity directly, and indirectly, by observing the men in my life. I also absorbed lessons from my mother. She is an incredible human being and the strongest person I know. She worked tirelessly to provide my siblings and me with all that our hearts desired. A very loving, progressive, and spiritually grounded woman, her strength at times manifested in a form of tough love. I recognize now that was her way of raising a man. Her lessons in tough love were an effort to overcompensate for the absence of a positive father figure in our home, but what I needed was a softer love.

The hurt male psyche is a reminder of the fractured, neglected boyishness many Latinx men may have lived through. As adolescent boys we were taught not to cry and "man up." We were encouraged to numb our pain in ways which lead to our emotional repression – a violent hardening process which extinguished the light, vulnerability, and empathy we might lack.

Which of us are still boys running around in grown men's bodies?

To this day, I struggle to show emotion, though I am a very sensitive man. I am afraid of intimacy for fear of being hurt. I have contributed to the destruction of love because of my misguided sense of righteousness. But I have grown, and I have learned to accept my flaws.

I have opened my heart to give and receive love. I have also forgiven myself and others for instances in which we did not recognize the Godliness in one another. I've learned just because you do not subscribe to traditional gender roles, it does not mean you are not *machista,* a male chauvinist. Knowing how to cook and clean for yourself is no excuse for your homophobia and womanizing. Just because you do not call a women a "bi---" or a "hoe" does not excuse your behaviors when you treat her that way. The subtle ways in which we tolerate harmful actions are just as damaging as its visible displays.

My stepfather's anger and his treatment of my mother was a result of his inability to express his deepest pain. Perhaps he didn't know how to, or was never given the space to do so. My mother's tough love was her way of preparing me to face the harshness of a world which does not embrace young Black boys. Perhaps she put up with an abusive man because on some level she had no choice but to "take the good with the bad." Both were victims of a culture which normalized their behaviors. It is our responsibility to change that narrative.

Here is our challenge: we must begin to establish new rites of passage for young men to embrace vulnerability, intimacy, and sensitivity. Maybe we need something other than rites or norms which boys are forced to adhere to? Maybe we need the freedom to become the best version of the humans we know ourselves to be? Maybe we do not need passages, traditional routes to travel, but instead require space to maroon, to break free altogether?

But I do know we deserve not to lose our playfulness, innocence, and curiosity; virtues which constitute healthier forms of masculinity. I know we need to stop telling boys to man up and hold their tears. I know we must help boys understand the beauty and equity present in potential partnerships with girls, instead of encouraging them to look at girls as objects to conquer in the home, on the streets, in the club, at the church house, and workplace. I know they deserve examples of what healthy relationships look like. And I know men must reinforce the importance of respect for others and ourselves.

It's okay for boys and men to FEEL. If we can agree with that point then perhaps we can continue healing ourselves and begin breaking down the negative effects of machismo and patriarchy.

CONNECTING THE DOTS
by Monte J. Wolfe

Retracing your steps can be a tricky process. Especially when you don't know what you're doing. That's how I would describe the first 33 years of my life. When I began seeing a therapist it was after having been diagnosed HIV-positive a little less than four years earlier in November of 2004. None of the first few years of living with HIV or disclosing it to those closest to me – was what I would refer to as easy.

By that point, although my health was good overall, my infectious disease specialist at the time suggested I seriously consider seeing a therapist as I was about to begin treatment to get my HIV numbers (viral load) to what is referred to as "undetectable."

Looking back, I can admit just how frightening a time it was for me, primarily because it represented a deeper level of realization about the reality of my newfound diagnosis. Fears not withstanding I moved forward with the decision to begin therapy in March of 2008; the truth is my life hasn't been the same since, which as far as I'm concerned is a good thing.

Outside of remembering what the office space looked like, there's not much I recall about my first therapy session. But I do remember being nervous and anxious since I had never done it before. At the same time, I recall feeling a sense of comfort knowing this professional was also a Black gay man who was only a few years older than me. Fortunately, I had been referred to him as a result of my involvement with the DC community-based organization, Us Helping Us. People Into Living (UHUPIL), which was an invaluable source of support at the time.

The last thing I definitely recall about my early days of therapy is how quickly 50 minutes seemed to fly by. Things would always start off slow, in terms of me opening up, and before I knew it, I'd blink and just as I felt we were "getting somewhere," it would be time to stop. This pattern continues pretty often to this day, some 12 years later, which over the years I've learned to find both the irony and humor in.

As I continued seeing a therapist regularly, not only did I find it useful, but also I began to look forward to our sessions. For the rest of that first year, no matter what was going on in my life – good, bad, or in between – I quickly began to see the benefit of having a licensed professional to talk with on a regular basis.

In the four walls of my therapist's office, I felt safe and was encouraged to dissect, examine, and unpack whatever issues were present and in the forefront of my mind each week. This is not to suggest the process was simple or was without its challenges. I remember someone asking me very early on in the process how it all was going and to this day, I vividly remember my response, *"Don't go out in the rain if you don't wanna get WET."*

To this day, I stand by that principle anytime someone would inquire about my feelings regarding seeing a therapist, which is, indeed, a process. Talking about my innermost thoughts in such a manner requires courage, trust, patience, and most of all, willingness. From the very beginning I wanted it all to work and for it all to be of some use to me, so once I was able to get clear about what to expect and what was expected of me, I was able to fully "buy into it," and do the work of healing.

While I've definitely become an advocate for therapy, I am in no way attempting to romanticize the process because as I learned within that first year, it can, at times, be profusely difficult to unravel all of the mental and emotional baggage we inevitably carry most of our lives. For me, like many others I've traded stories with – the baggage of which I speak is rooted in our past and the early formative years of growing up as children.

Although I never shied away from talking about my parents and my childhood, I didn't think it would play such a huge part in making sense of my adult life – until I started therapy. But it's where that first year landed me; right in the middle of a great pile of my very own memories, feelings, and muck which my then therapist helped me begin the process of sifting through.

The combination of seeing a skilled professional and me being in an open enough mental and emotional headspace to face unfamiliar territory marked a significant turning point in my life at age 33, in 2008.

I've been in therapy for 12 years now, give or take. I lapsed for nearly two years due to changes in jobs, insurance, and access to care. And, I've partnered with three different therapists. As I continue to move through the process today, I do so with a completely new, unique - and frightening – set of challenges before me, due to COVID-19.

I realize the only constant dynamic in this mental health journey of therapy has been the one person I was so prone to neglect prior beginning this process: my inner child. It was him all along; the little boy with fears, abandonment issues, insecurities, a big heart, and most of all, a voice I had to learn how to listen and pay attention to. It was always him I had to remember to love unconditionally. I had to unlearn all those thoughts, ideas, and beliefs I picked up along the way, which may not have been meant for me to carry.

MENTAL HEALTH ISSUES AMONG BLACK MEN
by Jeff Rocker

Complications due to COVID-19 adversely impact the Mental Health of Black Men

The coronavirus disease has adversely impacted the mental health of Black men in a myriad of ways. 2020 has brought a lot of pain, suffering and frustration to many Black men which has heightened their anxiety to new levels. An inordinate number of Black men find themselves constantly worrying about the safety of their families, financial stability, as well as reevaluating their short term and long term goals.

Sadly enough, research shows 44% of African Americans have experienced pay cuts or job losses, while 73% lack emergenc financial reserves to manage three months of expenses due to the pandemic. These alarming statistics reveal the significant decrease in household income imposed a substantial financial burden on Black men as they try to provide for their families.

To make matters worse, African Americans recorded the highest COVID-19 hospitalizations and death rates. This devastating situation attributes to increased chronic health conditions, poverty and racial discrimination which endangers their wellbeing. In order words, *"it's tough being a Black man in today's society but they don't have to deal with their issues on their own."*

Factors which deter Black Men from seeking help

Many Black men refrain from pursuing professional help due to various reasons. These barriers include finding therapists who are knowledgeable about Black culture, false representations or negative generalizations of therapy, fear of being judged and being misdiagnosed. For example, some mental health professionals harbor biased and negative perceptions – which influence them to misdiagnose Black men with mental illnesses such as schizophrenia, while, conversely, diagnosing White males with similar symptoms as experiencing mild mood disorders.

Culturally unskilled therapists discourage Black men from enrolling in counseling sessions; they fear clinicians may incorrectly diagnose them with mental illness they don't have. The fear of judgment hampers Black men from seeking help. Also, conventional masculinity beliefs can force men to endure unpleasant challenges: fear of their families identifying them as "crazy" due to their mental health diagnoses elevate their resistance to psychological assistance.

The negative depiction of counseling sessions in movies and television impede Black men from seeking help. For dramatization purposes, filmmakers often portray mental health patients as unpredictably violent, while depicting counselors as unethical or unhelpful. Hence, these factors can hinder Black men from pursuing professional assistance.

Black Men's Attitudes towards Mental Health

Faithfully, I believe the attitudes of Black men towards mental health is heading in the right direction. More African American therapists have received commendations from the public for helping their communities through innovative therapeutic approaches. Since the recent death of George Floyd, an unarmed Black man killed by a White male police officer, mental health agencies have been forced to hire more Black therapists to deal with the vicarious trauma experienced in the Black community.

There has been a huge void for Black mental health professionals for decades. It feels like our community is making notable progress today. In fact, the public admissions of Black male celebrities such as Dwayne "The Rock" Johnson, Brandon Marshall, Trevor Noah and Metta World Peace coping with their mental health issues and helping others do the same inspired countless other Black men to change their attitude towards mental health.

Unlike in the past, where African Americans viewed dialogue regarding mental health as an embarrassment, Black families are openly discussing psychological wellbeing issues. As a Celebrity Therapist, this is why I focus the majority of my time discussing mental health issues prevalent in the Black community and offering coping skills to overcome them. Black people need to continue these conversations among each other to promote mental health awareness.

Causes of Increased Suicide Cases among Young Black Men

Suicide rates among Black youth continue to increase exponentially due to various reasons. First and foremost, traumatic experiences instigated by massive killings of Black men by White male police officers impacts the suicide rates in young Black men. From 1991 to 2017, incidences of suicide among Black adolescents increased by 73% due to exposure to racial discrimination and violence, which fosters depression and stress.

Additionally, the integration of masculinity and racial norms, which mandate Black men to develop emotional resilience, triggers suicidal thoughts – especially when they fail to withhold their feelings. The lack of social relations or emotional support from peers has impacted suicide rates drastically in young Black teens.

At the same time, the lack of health insurance and high treatment expenditures hampers Black families from enrolling their children in counseling sessions. Therefore, our society needs to provide more culturally competent resources and programs in place to offset the issues which contribute to the inflating cases of suicide among Black adolescents.

KEEPING OLDER HIV+ BLACK GAY & BISEXUAL MEN IN MIND

by Craig Washington

"I want to live the rest of my life with an energy that ignites and irritates, burns and bubbles, soothes and inspires until it bursts from the atmosphere, dissipating into the cosmos."

– Craig G. Harris, I'm Going Out Like A F***ing Meteor.

What do older HIV+ Black gay and bisexual men (BGBM) need to sustain mental and emotional health and wellness? What key stressors impair their functioning and rob their fulfilment? What forces make them susceptible to these stressors? They endure universal life tolls of illness, injury, loneliness, loss, and rejection. They weather the same health afflictions and altering transitions as other elders.

These challenges may be compounded by chronic HIV infection and HIV-related physical and mental health conditions. They are more likely than their privileged counterparts to live on less than enough, lack stable housing, bounce in and out of care, be out of meds and have no one to call who cares. They are much more likely to live alone and have outlived their peer networks.

Social isolation is a top predictor strongly associated with poor health outcomes and dimmed life satisfaction. Research suggests strong correlations between depression, anger, and lack of perceived social support among older HIV+ Black adults1. Mental and emotional wellness for elder HIV+ Black gay men can be supported by the expansion of accessible social networks.

"The ubiquity of contexts within which stigmatization takes place suggests the existence of an underlying, antecedent social structure that extends beyond the borders of the Black and LGBT communities that are typically the focus of discussions of stigma among Black MSM."2

HIV+ BGBM 50+ experience stigma and discrimination based on their race, sexual orientation, gender presentation, age, and HIV status. Systemic racism relegates Black people to poverty, unemployment, homelessness and housing insecurity, and substandard health care. These factors are intensifies with the geometric marginalization of age, race, HIV status, sexuality and gender expressions and cultures outside of heteronormative bounds.

Many elder gay men are punished for the perceived failure to comply with gender and sexual norms. As kids they are programmed to believe something is wrong with them. *"Whenever an uncle or someone saw me with a doll it was snatched away. I was told boys don't do that,"* Khalid Idawu, 57, remembers.

Older cousins called Idawu "sissy" and physically abused him. Ulester Douglas, LMSW points out such alienating treatment is first inflicted by the family of origin. Douglas notes, *"We are asked 'What is wrong with you?' we are told 'you are the problem.' Many of us have internalized this, so much of the absence of wellness come from that."*

These beliefs, while instilled during early childhood and adolescent years, may persist if they are not rejected and supplanted by affirming concepts of HIV+ Black gay men's full selves.

"I had never seen guys dancing with guys, guys kissing. I felt like this is my world. I stopped thinking of myself as dirty. This is where I need to be. It changed my outlook on sin. I threw away the whole idea of sin."
– Renard Prather, 57, recalling his first time at a gay bar.

Douglas defines mental and emotional wellness as the ability to *"psychologically, emotionally and physically function within cultural norms,"* as well as the ability to *"find peace, take care of basic needs and navigate all those spaces."* He identifies the imposition of oppression (*"What is wrong with you?"*) as the point of distress.

In turn, the prevailing message of mental and emotional wellness is *"I am clear I am not the problem. And I'm going to do all I can to recognize that I am who I am."* Douglas asserts, for older HIV+ BGBM, mental wellness is, in itself, a rejection of insisting *"you are the problem."*

Many who internalized such negativity find affirmation through involvement in Black LGBTQ community. Exposure to affirming community within private networks, places of worship, discos, clubs, bathhouses, or other social spaces counters the belief they are "the problem."

Trauma is an overarching condition often overlooked among Blacks, specifically older HIV+ BGBM – and their unique trauma is not exclusively related to HIV status. The burden of the AIDS pandemic in the U.S. and internationally was a racialized phenomenon and the HIV-related stigma experienced by BGBM is a derivative of anti-Black and anti-gay animus.

At 50+ years of age, BGBM are long-term HIV survivors whether diagnosed 30 years or three weeks ago. Having lived over half a century, BGBM are survivors of the structural abuse meted by institutional racism and homophobia. But the havoc BGBM endured in the 80's was unlike anything they ever went through.

They endured the psychic cataclysm of seeing friends eaten away by alien infections, wiping up the once-popular hunk's shit and puke, keeping up with hospital visits, obits, funerals, and vigils, along with the infections and fears which racked their own bodies.

There was no definitive experience. For those who survived the worst of AIDS, what effects did it have on folks' sense of worth and belonging? How many fell into functional shock, without their pain articulated or acknowledged? BGBM who harbor anger, depression, and untreated trauma are less able to sustain or recreate friendships or romantic relationships. Those who are isolated are not as successful with their HIV drug adherence, self-care, or viral load suppression.

Many BGBM share accounts of stigmatizing treatment from the institutions charged with their care. Mythic tropes of predatory HIV+ men who infect others intentionally are (still) commonly espoused as if universally true. Dating and hook up apps are loaded with hostile commentary about HIV+ gay men from other gay men. The culpability of HIV+ BGBM is the central purpose of the 'down low' myth and primary justification for HIV criminalization. Such biases may lead older BGBM to withdraw given the multiple fronts of rejections they encounter.

Spirituality is an indispensable coping tool for many elders living with HIV. In his research paper "Experiences of Stigma and Spirituality of Older Black Men Living with HIV" (2019) Warren J. Muller summarized, *feeling empowered by spirituality allowed the participants to advocate and be kind* to themselves, handle challenging situations with psychosocial issues such as housing, mental health and employment issues."3

Through his liberated faith Claude Everett got self-acceptance: *"I had to step away from religion and find first my Creator in my own words and connect to that based on my life experience."* The stigma related to aging for HIV+ BGBM can be a relentless driver of isolation. Douglas observed, *"Gay men have also internalized a lot of that stuff around youth beauty and attractiveness, desirability, similar to how women have. Aging really brings that into focus."*

"When HIV+ Black gay men mature we tend to go into our shell. We look at younger, newer models of men. They are shiny, bright, and tight. We say, 'this is how I used to be.' We start to retreat." – Joe Robinson, 60.

As BGBM grow older they are edged out from the town square they were once welcomed, desired, included, or, at the very least, seen. Bars, clubs, and public events cater to the young without reflecting the tastes and styles of elders. Desirability is a premium commodity in gay male culture everywhere. As physical beauty shifts, elders may encounter multiple losses of attention, desirability, social connection, and self-esteem. Douglas remarked, *"Those are some of the issues that older Black gay men are contending with, all in the contexts of racism, heterosexism, intersecting with class. That's a lot to navigate."*

"I kept hearing about older Black gay men being more and more isolated," recalls Malcolm Reid. He serves as Program Manager for the Silver Lining Project, a program of THRIVE SS (Transforming HIV Resentment Into Victories Everlasting Support Services), an advocacy organization for HIV+ BGM in Atlanta. The Silver Lining Project focuses on men 50 and older.

Once introduced to THRIVE SS, Reid told co-founder Larry Scott-Walker he wanted to do something for guys his age. Other elder members asked for more emphasis on their age-related concerns and interests. Scott-Walker gave the green light and Reid responded by organizing a support group: Mature Men of Color. The group's popularity expanded when it launched a Facebook group, and with the help of grant funding evolved into The Silver Lining Project.

Since its inception the Silver Lining Project has given older HIV+ BGBM opportunities for ongoing fellowship and community involvement. Monthly meetings such as the Obas Roundtable afford members the chance to share space custom fit for them. An online advocacy education series explores HIV and Aging, PTSD and Trauma, Loss and Transition, and Stigma. Designed as an anti-stigma campaign, a 2019 photo shoot featuring members in classic black and white shots made a transgressive visual statement.

Social distancing due to the COVID-19 pandemic heightens the risk of increased isolation, depression, and anxiety for older BGBM. Elders may find it difficult to adapt to virtual socializing and the increased dependencies on current technology and social media to stay in touch. There is no more critical time to have more BGBM engaged in therapy. Through a collaboration between THRIVE SS and a local counseling center, members receive free telehealth counseling.

"Life was just being, doing everyday activities, and just making it through. I was disconnected from intimacy with anybody," said Renaldo George, 53. In 2015 he enrolled in an outpatient program at Positive Impact Health Centers. His therapist helped him cope with feelings he normally avoided – including his sexuality and abandonment by his birth mother. *"It helped me feel validated. It provided me connection. I just needed to feel some connection,"* George said.

There is little doubt about the correlation between the strength of social systems and mental wellness. First and foremost, an increased investment in this population from within and outside of Black LGBTQ community is overdue. Recognition of the benefits of social intimacy can inform and influence advocacy efforts, health policy, housing, and HIV health interventions. More mental health clinicians can be trained and enlisted to treat elder BGBM.

Campaigns and other strategies can be developed to promoted social connection as a lifeline. Organic resources – clbs and retreats – to draw intergenerational and older crowds provide important models for this challenge. The generation who has contributed so much to develop communities and services enjoyed by successive generations deserved to be kept in mind and held in community, lovingly and fiercely.

Throughout existing research there is a stunning dearth of knowledge about the lives of older BGBM living with HIV. Additional culturally competent research to consider how social resources can save and enhance the quality of lives of colder HIV+ BGBM is sorely needed. The experiences, adaptations, resiliencies, and wisdom of older BGBM must be explored in future studies. An increased focus on this neglected population will yield immeasurable contributions for research, health policy and practice, social justice, and other fields.

References

1. Nicole Ennis Whitehead, Ph.D., Lauren E. Hearn, MS and Larry Burrel, MS (2014); The Association between Depressive Symptoms, Anger and Perceived Support Resources among Underserved Older HIV Positive Black/African American Adults, AIDS Patient Care and STDs Volume 28, Number 9, 2014, DOI: 10.1089/apc.2014.0126.

2. Rahwa Halle, Mark B. Padilla, and Edith A. Parker (2011) "Stuck in the Quagmire of an HIV Ghetto": The meaning of stigma in the lives of older Black gay and bisexual men living with HIV in New York City, Cult Health Sex. 2011 April; 13 (4): 4290442 DOI: 10.1080/13691058.2010.537769.

3. Warren L. Miller Jr. (2019); Experiences of Stigma and Spirituality of Older Black Men Living with HIV, Journal of Social Service Research, DOI: 10.1080/01488376.2019.158451.

OUTRAGE ON THE FRONT PAGE
by Ayoinmotion

The pain never goes away. It seeps through like blood running down from a wound. This wound is deep. So deep that the blood trickles and runs just like I do. You see for some of us we know the pain like its friendship, but for others it's marriage with divorce an impossibility. So, I have to wonder: how does heaven deal with an overflow of souls arriving before their time?

Way ahead of schedule because they were victims of the evil that men do.

It's hardly breaking news that the value of black lives is in tatters. With the release of the newest viral video, the anger spirals. We pick up placards calling for justice because we are tired of living in a hospice; I mean, living in a country where the authorities stay asleep to the fact that parents are planning their children's wake. No disrespect but I don't need y'all telling me to stay woke. I am not in a coma. Our dead bodies are not meant to be exhibited like a gallery at the MOMA – this is real life!

We protest in anger at those meant to protect and serve, because them hunting us is really nothing new, just a **sad precedent**. It's backward, like watching the Secret Service kill the President. And the media, well they swarm the scene like a honeycomb with bees. You see them running commentary on the battles between both sides. It feels like a game. And in games, they call plays. And plays, well, they are scripted. And in this one everyone plays their role so well, even the grand jury delivers the same line of not guilty. When the glove fits, they still acquit. When there's video, they still don't convict.

Our outrage is just a story on the front page. We need to do more than just talk if we want change. We can't move on because Erica Garner can't. Diamond Reynolds can't. Sandra Bland can't. I say her name because although we empathize deeply, grief is not a friend that shares your couch, it's more like a lover that cuddles with you in your arms. Waking you up like insistent snoring or sirens at 3:00 am, you don't get to run away from grief.

After each protest we go back to the cycle of living our lives. Like we did when Amadou Diallo died. Like we did when Eric Garner died. Like we did when Oscar Grant, Alton Sterling and Philandro Castile died. **Their** names reeled off like a film only that in this real life so what good is a wave of outrage without sustained action? So, join me in running, whether you are black, white, or any color under the sun, we should all be running; not away from the issue but to actually changing it. We can't keep treating police brutality like a substitute teacher when it's in fact the Principal.

Racial police profiling, stop-and-frisk, harassment, and other variations of systemic oppression aren't new just more viral. We were being capped before Kaepernick and change will require us to stay on the issue and not vote for mayors, presidents and other politicians that play lip service but drive away from this issue like a car service.

We need to make them implement laws that matter, **laws that hold law enforcement officials who use unnecessary force accountable, laws that don't justify every force by the police as necessary when it isn't. Laws that address the blatant or sometimes invincible systemic** racism that is interwoven into the very fabric of America's psyche.

Training that acknowledges that some of us have had experiences with the institution of protect and serve has left us feeling more like 3/5 of a man? So don't minimize my trauma by telling me those were just bad apples or attempt to appease our anger with a passive admission of an inept system, that's not enough. Listen, it's not about blue versus black but we keep getting killed in a way that feels like them versus us.

How many more parents need to attend their children's wake? How many more America? How many more Am-Erica's Garner need to come home without Eric? How many more viral videos, how many more on the front page?

So, till it stops, I am running. Running to her even if society tries to stop me and tells me to move on. Even if the viral videos cause trauma that feels so all consuming. I am running to her because I have to. We all have to say her name and say his name till we don't have to anymore. The victims and families of police brutality and unnecessary violence can't fade the pain away. **So even when the protests, press, and outrage on the front page fade away, the pain never does.**

LOVING THROUGH OUR TRAUMA, PART ONE
by Jonathan Mathias Lassiter, Ph.D.

An acquaintance recently commented, *"American Black men can't love because they are psychically damaged."* I was immediately offended; what I heard was, "here's another reason Black men are deficient, pathological, etc."

I flat out rejected his extreme emotion. I soon began analyzing my reaction. Why was I so insulted? Was he right? I decided before I ended my relationship with him altogether, I should give his comment more thought. I started by assessing the veracity of his assertions: 1) American Black men can't love; and 2) American Black men are psychically damaged.

First, *I* know Black men can and do love. That's not debatable. However, are the ways in which many Black men love healthy? Well, they could be healthier. bell hooks wrote in <u>We Real Cool: Black Men and Masculinity</u> *"Black boys are often victims of soul murder because they are taught by Black parents only patriarchal modes of expression (stoicism, toughness, e.g.) are acceptable."*

Black boys often learn they must suppress their feelings, creativity, and authentic voices to be "real men" and, in some cases, "safe" from emotional humiliation or physical harm. This restrictive parenting is partly in response to heteropatriarchy and white supremacy – which limits the ways of being for *all* Black people.

Historically, Black men have been denied access to traditional means of manhood (protecting one's family from physical and social injury, success in capitalist markets, e.g.) and pathologized for embracing encouraged and expected to demonstrate manliness via dominance, emotional suppression, and sexual aggression: with the exception of violent aggression.

Thus, many Black men show their love from a distance by material means and sexual attention. For example, my father once shared, *"My Dad loved me. But he never said it. He showed he loved me by going out and working all day. But then he would come home, give my mama money for the bills, get dressed, and take the rest of the money and go down to the juke joint and sit and drink with the other men...we didn't talk in those days like I talk to you."*

Secondly, are Black men psychically damaged? The short answer is not more than anyone else. But it's important to recognize this distinct fact: Black people have suffered centuries of white supremacist and other forms of oppressive terror (classism, heteropatriarchy, e.g.) alongside detachment or mistreatment from Black parents.

These inhumane experiences constitute trauma, which painfully impacts the way people think and behave. Two poignant dynamics might explain the effects of trauma, as it relates to how Black men love: 1) avoidance of situations which make them feel vulnerable; 2) negative changes in emotions and thoughts impact the way people think about their future and their relationships (foreshortened, and dulls positive emotions like joy and love, e.g.).

There are some Black same-gender-loving (SGL) men who police the femininity in other Black SGL men whom they encounter. I remember being dismissed by a Black man because I was *"too feminine"* and he thought if we socialized together in public, other people would assume he, too, was SGL because I was *"faggoty."*

Sadly, his response to a lifetime of homonegativity was to distance himself from a potentially loving relationship because it would render him emotionally vulnerable to heteropatriarchal malevolence. From my view, his mental health had been negatively affected by the recurring trauma of Black male oppression.

Yes, it's true some Black men express their love through less-than-optimal methods and the mental health of some Black men is tarnished by oppression. Nonetheless, I still reject the racist notion Black men can't love. I am loved by my Black male friends and I give my love to others every day.

However, as Black men, we can learn, through personal example,to find ways to love outside of the heteropatriarchal, white male gaze. Black men can learn to cultivate the spirit of courage in a system which does znot reward our beauty, boldness, and brilliance. I'm asking Black men today: what do these creative manners of love look like, and how do we actualize them?

LOVING THROUGH OUR TRAUMA, PART TWO
by Jonathan Mathias Lassiter, Ph.D.

Before we, as Black men, love others, we must first love ourselves. Loving through our trauma requires we: 1) acknowledge our privileges and how we use them; 2) embrace femininity and vulnerability; and 3) purge ourselves of internalized white supremacy.

Our society has a built-in system of gendered economic and racial oppression of privilege. We take privilege (based on class, education, gender, heterosexual orientation, e.g.) for granted and do not recognize our responsibility to use them for empowerment, not marginalization.

Privilege can sometimes unconsciously contribute to dominating and silencing people closest to us (Black children and women, e.g.). Black men who participate in systems of gender oppression are offered few rewards in those systems, even when there is a perception of gaining power.

But what good is gaining power if it hurts the people we claim to love? Writer Toni Morrison said, *"If you can only be tall because somebody is on their knees, then you have a serious problem. And my feeling is, white people have a very, very serious problem and they should start thinking about what they can do about it. Take me out of it."* We must check our privileges.

Black men, in my opinion, will never be whole until we embrace and harness the feminine energy inside us. Male supremacy and effemiphobia keeps us in boxes restricted by gender norms dictating to us being emotionally effusive or nurturing is something "real men" avoid.

Boys are taught artistic and creative pursuits are "for girls." We value physically and shaming peers who don't meet the standards of corporeal prowess. We are restricted in our fashion, and other modes of interpersonal expression not centered on competition and physical activity. Yet women's relationships are centered on emotional processing and career choices.

Black men are often hypervigilant with our mannerisms and others' gender violations. A rejection of femininity and its associate traits (cooperativeness, e.g.) compromises our human potential for wholeness. We tend to operate from emotional deserts – and we're afraid to ask for the help and love we need.

Sometimes Black men are paranoid of their vulnerability and will punish others who make them feel vulnerable. In my father's humble attempt to protect me, I was often told *"stop crying,"* or, *"toughen up."* From his perspective, an emotionally delicate or expressive Black man was an endangered one.

The isolating and self-destructing rejection of femininity is compounded by white supremacy. In fact, white supremacy renders Black people worthless in white societal domains. Also, white supremacy further divides Black men and Black women by convincing Black men, Black women emasculate us and make it difficult for us to achieve economic and social progress.

White supremacy views Black men as dangerous, while simultaneously making us feel unsafe due to environmental racism, mass incarceration and police violence. Black men are encouraged to be aggressive, punished for minor transgressions, and ridiculed for being vulnerable.

Furthermore, white supremacy limits our human sexual expressions. For example, Black men are often seen as sexually dominant (aggressive, or "tops" e.g.) but are soon embraced or rejected for how well they "perform" racist stereotypes of sexuality. Patriarchal norms and racial tropes restrict Black men and their various modes of beingness.

As Black men, we must liberate ourselves from the bondage of heteropatriarchy (a system which normalizes homonegativity) and white supremacy. If we are to be our authentic selves, we must retrain ourselves to be vulnerable and value intimacy (beyond sexual intercourse).

We can love through our trauma by:

1. Affirming our value as human beings. If your maleness was taken, who would you be? If your ability to make money was taken, who would you be? Look in the mirror and find something lovable about the person without any privileges.
2. Keep a daily list of three things you like about yourself not based on externals.
3. Make space for alone time with yourself in silence. We must learn to celebrate and tolerate ourselves by ourselves.
4. Try and practice mindful meditation, where you focus on the sensations of your own body or your breath – and nothing else.
5. Seek out social support from people who actively encourage your vulnerability, and don't fight their efforts to help you. Vulnerability is not about being weak. To be vulnerable is

about becoming (emotionally and mentally) strong through our human connection.

6. Start a conversation with someone you trust and share a vulnerable emotion you felt at least once a week.

7. Acknowledge we have privileges (whether based on cisgender male body status, class, or education) we sometimes (consciously or subconsciously) use to empower ourselves at the expense of disempowering others.

8. Complete **The Black Male Privilege Checklist.**
   - Ask yourself: Are my interactions with others mostly from a distance?
   - Do I have close friends (besides female partners) who I discuss my emotions?
   - Do I tend to talk negatively in—or avoid—conversations with men I deem effeminate?
   - As a Black SGL man, do I try hiding my femininity in public, or avoid effeminate men?

9. Use your experiences of patriarchal and racial trauma and learn to cultivate genuine empathy for other oppressed people. Affirming the humanity in others liberates our own.

10. For example, speak up for the women in your life at home, at school, at work.

11. And, hold your sister accountable for telling your nephew to "stop being a punk."

KEEP BREATHING: THE ROAD TO RECOVERY FOR AN ALABAMA TAR HEEL

by Myles J. Robinson

This has been the most challenging decade of my life. I struggled with anxiety, depression, loneliness, and suicidal thoughts since August 2012. I graduated from high school and received a full scholarship to the college of my dreams: The University of North Carolina (UNC) at Chapel Hill. But to my surprise and ultimate dismay, I was simultaneously headed for the brightest highs and darkest lows imaginable.

In college I became a global traveler. Visiting China and Costa Rica exposed me to different cultures and different people I still cherish today. I also went to the Summer Olympics in Rio de Janeiro, Brazil, where I felt my heart shine in ways indescribable. But later, I harbored some ugly confusion. I felt dark inside; my depression, loneliness, and suicidal thoughts hurt.

I can recall the joyous feeling of apparent invincibility after I received my full college scholarship, traveling around the world and interning at my dream workplaces. I can also recall the painful feeling of anxiety upon reaching the invisible ceiling of success I painted in my head – and the depression, which swallowed my spirit. It took years to acknowledge my outward arrogance and inward entitlement, which masked deeply hidden insecurities.

I vividly remember how empty my soul felt due to an unfulfilling relationship with God and my lack of a church home in college. UNC was 500 miles away from my family in Birmingham, Alabama. Sadly, I had a difficult time admitting I needed help, keeping everything "together" every day, and understanding my conflicting emotions.

I was in desperate need of something...anything.

In 2015, I left school and isolated myself for years. I reached a low I pray my enemies will never experience. Through grace, I learned to cultivate faith in a loving God. I'm thankful for the many friendships and meaningful relationships which challenge the essence of my inner being. I'm proud of the people in my life, near and far, who keep me accountable, grounded and inspired.

My last suicide attempt was one year ago. I was at the Denver International Airport on May 27 when I distinctly heard God's audible voice. He met me exactly where I was in the valley. He did something for me – and it still makes me cry today. He instilled peace.

If you are reading my story and struggling with your mental health, can I encourage you?

KEEP BREATHING

Every moment we decide to keep breathing moves us closer to our breakthrough. The healing process is an individual journey and different for everyone. Nevertheless, we are strong when we confess our struggles to one another.

Morning affirmations help me on my journey. I remind myself this every day. I am a special individual who makes the world smile being here. I can be a masterpiece and a work in process. As I seek to keep breathing, I also want to be gentler with myself.

This decade has defined me. I learned one thing for sure: it is possible to chase your dreams and reinvent your life. During my recovery, I began a personal assessment and self-inventory of my emotions and feelings. Many of my journal entries included letters of self-encouragement.

Listed below are poignant examples of my self-awareness from the last seven years:

- *Failure leads to the greatest success: humility and learning. Success leads to the greatest failure pride.*
- *Everyone has two valuable gifts: our mind and our timer. Our happiness and success in life is contingent upon what we do with both gifts.*
- *Peace is not the absence of inner conflict. Inner conflict is not the absence of peace.*
- *We will never leave where we are until we decide where we would rather be.*
- *We remain humble by acknowledging the seeds of failure in every success.*
- *We remain hopeful by acknowledging the seeds of success in every failure.*

- *Nothing gold can stay; nothing black does either.*
- *Personal growth can feel like being lost. It is okay to feel lost. People tend to grow more when they are lost than when they are on a straight path with a clear view of where they are going.*
- *Other people's road maps will not be able to guide you, but they can show you how to draw your own road map.*
- *The night is always darkest before dawn.*
- *Feelings are overrated: actions heal us, and feelings hurt us.*

Some of the important examples of positive mental health for me today are meditation, prayer, smiling and stretching. Breathing is a foundational exercise which has been transformative lately. I encourage you to find your own routine and develop your own habits. Change begins with the first step. Let us keep growing together.

I love you, and God loves you even more.

BLACK MEN SHOULD ONLY CRY SOMETIMES

by Dr. Obari Cartman

In November 2017 singer and actor Tyrese couldn't see his 10 years-old daughter for a few months because his co-parent issued a restraining order. Tyrese was so distraught he posed a video of himself crying. I had empathy watching him because three days is the longest amount of time I can go without seeing my son before I become uneasy. However, a few months prior, I was embarrassed by videos of two Black male journalists, Van Jones and Gianno Caldwell, who cried on television in response to some racist comments made by President Donald Trump.

I viewed Jones and Caldwell as weak for crying.

If you read "weak" as "feminine," that's completely on you. I never said that. I don't think a crying man is more in touch with his feminine side. I see him more aligned with his human nature. My notion of the weak to strong spectrum has nothing to do with gender, and everything to do with power. I'm more likely to make an age comparison than a gender one. I'll never say, "man up, quit acting like a girl." But I will say, "you're a grown ass man, stop acting like a little boy."

Children are still learning to experience and appropriately express their emotions. I will never tell a child to deny their true feelings, but I do feel it's my parental responsibility to shape my sons' emotional expression. I give them all the love and support they need when they fall and hurt themselves. But when one cries because he can't have another cookie I won't hesitate to say, "boy quit crying and go drink some water."

I think the reason we cry matters. To be disappointed Trump said something racist suggests a level of unhealthy delusion. I don't think he warrants that kind of power in our minds. Did Jones and Caldwell expect more from their President? I can't imagine them being upset if they were prepared for his buffoonery. Maybe they expected dignity and leadership from him? That actually would be sad.

In 4:44, Jay-Z's most gangsta rap album yet, he said,

"I never wanted another woman to know
Something about me that you didn't know
I promised, I cried
I couldn't hold."

Did he cry because he got caught? Maybe that's harsh. I appreciate the vulnerability he expressed. Throughout his album there was a theme of how much pain he would feel if he lost his daughter, which I think opened him up to also feel the loss of his wife.

"Cry Jay-Z, we know the pain is real/But you can't heal what you never reveal."

Neal Brennan, a white male artist noted for his edgy writing on the critically-acclaimed Chappelle's Show, in his beautifully insightful stand-up comedy special on Netflix said, I actually think Black dudes appreciated how openly sad I was because Black dudes aren't allowed to be openly sad in public. The only way a Black dude can openly have sadness in public is if he does it with a saxophone."

The question is definitely about expression. We know Black men feel, despite their best attempts to hide it. We know Black men mask sadness and fear as anger. We know Black men self-medicate to not feel. It seems, however, without more nuanced direction around emotional expression young Black men will continue to dismiss the prevailing plea of our time: to reassess the building blocks of our masculinity from the ground up.

I sell a t-shirt which says, "Men cry..." The t-shirt gets a lot of scoff from Black men. While the message serves as a reminder to Black men and our humanity – and emotions are not a woman thing – it only works if it's effective. I'm wondering if we need to also teach crying sometimes doesn't mean crying all the time. Perhaps Black men have been holding it in so long they fear opening a flood gate? Black men also still have to survive the harsh realities of their block or board room.

I don't want a Black man to stop sobbing at work if his boss chastises him, but I also don't want him to pretend he wasn't hurt. I want him to recognize the shame in his body, to allow it to pierce him deeply, notice where it hits him in his abdomen, make a connection between that feeling and his fear of losing the security of a job, hold a straight face, keep eye contact, and get back to work – not drown his sorrows at a bar or strip club before he goes home.

I don't want a young Black man to think he has to cry in the middle of the cafeteria when an upperclassman makes fun of his shoes. Instead he should feel his chest pounding, eyes watering, try not to blink, take deep breaths, ride the L, force a smirk, walk slowly to a bathroom stall where he can sneak a muffle cry in his sleeve, and go back to class – not go to snapchat and tell his cousins to meet them after the last bell.

On the other hand, my younger brother has never seen me cry. I had no idea until he said it recently. It seems incredible to me because I cry all the time. There are songs, movies, and even some commercials which made me cry. I've cried so often because of our mother I can barely look her directly in the eye anymore. I can cry in an instant at the thought of my son getting hurt or dying.

I love crying.

I feel so much lighter after a good cry. It's not because I hold it in when I'm around my brother; it doesn't even come up. My instinct or man training or perceived duty to protect him from the burden of my pain makes it so I don't know if I'm capable of feeling that intensely in his presence. Sounds like a man box when I describe it that way. What lessons do young Black men learn if I only cry in my car alone? How will they even know it's okay?

Some men kill instead of crying. Themselves and others. We not gone change the entire culture of manhood overnight, but we can work more urgently to create safe and trusting spaces for Black men to gather and cry. Or just share. And we can teach Black men as soon as they can speak how to attach language to emotional experiences they naturally have.

We can teach the cleansing power of tears, encourage Black men to AT LEAST cry alone, and how to use the emotional signals our bodies give us to interrogate their source. We can teach Black men how to include the power of emotions as a part of decision making and successfully navigating the world as a Black man. It's a tough world for all of us. We are clear, trials and tribulations come with the job of being a Black man in America.

Crying should also be taught as a natural part of life for Black men, too. Sometimes.

THE AUTHENTIC THERAPIST

by Percival Fisher, Jr.

In his book titled, Black Men and Depression, author John Head says, "Depression denies our families and us the enjoyment of our achievement...it distorts our thinking so much that we refuse to accept our accomplishments as evidence of who we have become, and instead embrace society's negative stereotypes of us." (Head, 2004).

Head's perspective on depression – specifically from a Black man's perspective – is the best, in my opinion. He describes what I have been feeling for a large part of my childhood and, at times, as an adult. I consistently experience the following thoughts:

Am I capable enough?
Am I good enough?
Am I strong enough?
Am I man enough?

I regularly endure internal struggles and live with these daily thoughts as a young Black man in America. Conflicting thoughts are a normal part of my conscious experience as I seek to navigate life. I am 36 years old and I get bombarded daily with images, languages, and visuals of Black men who are demoted, devalued, disillusioned, disrespected, and emasculated by the very system which informs us we're equal to Black women, and the greater white society.

Every day, a racist system informs Black men we can achieve any dream through hard work and perseverance. However, what if (after) I worked hard and persevered I still have thoughts of doubt, sadness, and shame? This has been my internal struggle for many years, but I kept quiet, and muted the voice inside because I wanted to "man up," and make others feel comfortable when I was feeling ncomfortable.

For many years I kept painful feelings to myself because I felt I did not have an outlet, or a safe space or a voice to be my authentic self. This is my experience. I have been programmed by my community and the greater society to keep quiet about my internal struggles because I am a man. And, I ought to remain emotionally and physically "strong" to endure this experience called life or I am going to perish in silence.

I am 36 years-old African-American male who self-identifies as bisexual. I always thought my bisexuality was a curse: it is shameful and sinful to be bisexual and Black. Growing up I heard people say things like "it's an abomination," or "God don't like gays," or "God made Adam and Eve, not Adam and Steve." I had to learn how to cultivate self-love, first and foremost, and embrace all my "chocolate thunder" character, intellect, and style.

However, self-love did not come easy for me. Part of my struggle was coping with how my own community shamed me for being a (so-called) sexual minority, getting excellent grades in school, planning my future, having personal goals, and being articulate. I was hurt when folks would say to me, "why do you talk like that?' Or, some would say to me, "you sound white."

...but what does **that** mean?

Additionally, the leading white culture shames me for being a proud Black man. I am a highly educated, Ivy League graduate with a Masters' Degree, yet I experience "micro-aggressions" at work every day because some man or woman from the dominant culture does not accept me in their professional environment. They do not want me there - it makes them uncomfortable.

I am a Black man who does not fit the stereotypical brute, criminal, sex addict, or any other caricature in their minds to make them feel emotionally and socially unsafe. This is a paradox, a paradox once emotionally dark, lonely, and painful because I (had to) ask myself: who can I turn to when I experience these feelings? However, through the grace of God I am still here! I can share my story and possibly help someone.

When I became a Clinical Therapist, I wanted to make a difference. As a Licensed Clinical Social Worker (LCSW) and Board Certified Diplomate in Clinical Social Work, I intend to use my clinical training, professional experience, and self-worth to help other people of color, especially Black men, to offer a space where they feel heard, respected, and validated. I want to provide a space where folks can be their authentic selves: without judgment, ridicule, or shame.

Today, I am making a difference. I provide these services because I know from personal experience how difficult it is to find - and trust - a therapist; let alone a Black therapist. I provide services to help Black men and people of color, specifically, to engage in spaces they can feel emotionally vulnerable but also emotionally and physically safe.

Furthermore, I provide a space where they can share their cultural experiences, the Black experience, and know that I GET IT because I have been there. I am my client's keeper, and we share this experience together. I know how it feels to be treated different: like an outcast, unique, or weird. I know, through my personal experience, how it feels to endure anger, anxiety, bitterness, depression, doubt, loneliness, shame, and trauma.

When I work with my clients, I provide tools which can help them manage their presenting concerns and various symptoms. However, I not only provide them with coping tools but with genuine respect. I respect and treat clients how I want to be treated in our sessions. I am a Black male therapist. I am not the normal, super clinical, uptight, white-collar therapist.

Also, I like to model simple ways for my clients to be authentic. For example, I dress casually, and sport my dreadlocks to keep it 100! I believe therapy is designed to humbly meet people where they're at, provide a compassionate ear, learn about their story, demonstrate empathy, build on their strengths, and empower them with encouragement, love, and support. Therapy is truly a privilege and I am thankful to be part of this healing process.

Head, J (2004) Depression and Black Men: Saving our lives, healing our families and friends. Harlem Moon/Broadway Books.

A PERSONAL AND PROFESSIONAL JOURNEY WITH MENTAL HEALTH

by Terrence Coffie

My anxiety was running high.

I was standing on the stage of Radio City Music Hall in New York City at the 2017 Graduation Ceremony of New York University's Silver School of Social Work. I was there to receive my Master's Degree of Science in Social Work, and was humbly named the NYU's Alex Rosen N.A.S.W. (National Association of Social Workers) Student of the Year.

My anxiety was not solely because of my nervousness in receiving such a prestigious honor, but something much deeper. In my mind this evening, this award would finally "fix" everything. For many years I struggled with 'inadequacy disorder' (a self-diagnosed term highlighting my drive to achieve due to my lack of opportunity; sometimes inadequacy disorder made me feel, think, and display awkward social behaviors).

"The Black community suffers from an increased rate of mental health concerns, including anxiety and depression. The increased incidence of psychological difficulties in the Black community is related to the lack of access to appropriate and culturally responsive mental health care, prejudice and racism inherent in the daily environment of Black individuals, and historical trauma enacted on the Black community by the medical field." (Vance, 2019).

Since I have always felt this way about my life, I had to find a way to embrace it. As I stood on the stage next to Dr. Jean Anasta (the award presenter and former NASW President), I looked out into the audience of what seemed to be a sea of people – and it was the first time I began to believe I would now be considered normal.

While I listened to Dr. Anasta share about my illustrious academic career, my anxiety began to rise considerably. And, how ironic was it for Dr. Chirlane McCray, wife of NYC Mayor Bill Di Blasio, who introduced one of the most comprehensive mental health initiatives in the country, to be sitting right behind me?

As Dr. Anasta continue to highlight my career of being named a 2016 President's Award recipient; Excellence in Leadership Award recipient; my work with esteemed author and advocate Michelle Alexander, and a list of other accolades, even I was impressed. But despite her glowing remarks of my journey, I found myself wondering who was she talking about?

What the hell was I doing on this stage?

NUY made a mistake! I was unworthy of my accomplishments. I was a mistake. All my life I felt like a mistake. Somewhere on the assembly line of people, when God dispensed the basic fundamental aspects to create a human being, I was missing something. I was missing what makes a person whole, and I sought to hide, repair, and supplement this void my entire life.

My anxiety increasingly worsened. I feared being exposed, and worried everyone would soon discover I was a mistake. At that moment on the stage of Radio City Music Hall, as I was about to receive this prestigious award from the former NASW President, with the First Lady of New York City sitting directly behind me, and with all my family, friends, classmates, and colleagues in attendance, I feared I would fart! Don't fart, don't fart, don't fart, I said quietly to myself.

As humorous as this may sound, this coping mechanism is the distorted emotional reality I have endured my whole life. I told myself don't fart that evening, but other times it was the messages from people in my past I had internalized and would beat myself up inwardly with:

"You can't receive anything less than a C."
"Never say anything wrong."
"Walk straight."
"Sit up straight."
"Be polite."
"You better be good, never don't, you have to!"

I grew up striving to be perfect because I believed I was a mistake.

On that night, just like the ovies I watched in foster homes, I would be fixed. The brokenness I recognized in myself long ago would be repaired. Whatever I did not receive on the assembly line of life I would be given that night. But after receiving my award, after the perfunctory smile I learned to mimic over the years, after the cheers and congratulations of everyone, while walking back to my seat, I painfully realized I wasn't fixed.

My mind continued to demand perfection, even more so now. But I was broken, and deathly afraid. During my academic and professional career,

I was deemed exceptional, an anomaly of sorts: a success. I was recognized for my intelligence, commitment, drive, and passion. But how else could you describe a man who spent over 19 years of his life incarcerated, who grew up in foster homes, who was abandoned by his parents, who was mentally, physically, and sexually abused as a child – and born into poverty?

I spent my entire life wishing I was someone other than myself. I saw the good in everyone else but myself. Realistically, I didn't have a chance of amounting to anything but another statistic, like so many other Black and Brown young men in this country – to beat the odds! What else could I have been referred to, except, as exceptional?

Sadly, exceptional was not what I saw or believed for myself. The truth is my drive, passion, intelligence, and other attributes to describe me or my success were by-products of my fear of failure. My fear of failure demands perfection, even from a broken vessel. Throughout my life I was asked, "have you been diagnosed?" or, "have you dealt with the trauma of your childhood?" (I was asked this question mostly by white people).

Mental illness in my life, and in the environments I grew up in, was not acknowledged, discussed, or accepted as freely as it is in white America. Maladaptive behaviors or mental illness in the clinical sense, in poor Black and Brown communities, are non-existent, not because there isn't mental illness. Unfortunately, it wasn't culturally or socially acceptable; in fact, mental illness in the Black community is either ignored or criminalized by society, for obvious and sometimes not so obvious reasons.

I am speaking for myself.

I view mental illness as a privilege and luxury only afforded to white people. From Columbine to Sandy Hook shootings and many other incidents which involved whites, these individuals were considered "mentally disturbed" and somehow "failed' by society. And yet, in cases such as Steven Taylor, a 33 years-old Black man with a history of mental illness who was killed in a police-involved shooting, while holding a baseball bat in a San Leandro Walmart...

...as the late Tupac Shakur rapped, *"That's just the way it is."*

For people of color, the lack of mental health support, services, and/or investments in our communities is a testament to society's beliefs and lack of commitment to the Black community regarding mental health treatment. I have never discounted anyone's life experiences which resulted in trauma.

What I am attempting to express is a societal belief; Blacks are exempt from the conversation of mental illness, which has also been internalized by the Black community. Mental illness in Black communities have not only been internalized, but normalized. My breakthrough came two years after the evening of being named *NYU's NASW* Student of the Year, although in hindsight I realize I have been suffering from something my entire life.

I am currently using the Stages of Change Model in therapy for myself, which has six dynamics, and I fear the unknown. I feel apprehensive and skeptical, yet remain hopeful about my journey. My views of mental illness, the stigma in the Black community, and society's lack of understanding or acceptance influence my belief system.

According to the U.S. Department of Minority Health, in 2017, suicide rates for Black men were four times higher than Black women. Soul Train host and producer Don Cornelius, singer and songwriter Donny Hathaway, music executive Chris Lighty, NFL Hall of Famer Junior Seau, and actor Lee Thompson-Young died by suicide – each man suffered with mental health issues.

Only in recent years (which really feels like months) has dialogue about mental illness in the Black community taken place. Today, with celebrities like Snoop Dogg, Big Sean, and Kanye West publicly disclosing their mental health challenges and therapy sessions, national conversations have positively encouraged Black people to consider, seek and utilize treatment.

I hope this cultural trend for healing continues. Dr. Thomas A. Vance of Columbia University said, "The Black community exists at the intersection of racism, classism, and health inequity, their mental health needs are often exacerbated and mostly unfulfilled. Issues related to economic insecurity, and the associated experiences, such as violence and criminal injustice, further serve to compound the mental health disparities in the Black population."

Addressing Mental Health in the Black Community, Dr. Thomas Vance.
February 8, 2019.

TRANSFORMING THE PAIN WE HIDE
by Donnell Hill

The pain we hide is a killer.
The pain slowly eats away at every cell of our being as we move through
this life experience.
The pain hides behind smiles, false hope and niceness.

But beneath this black skin,
In the pit of this black soul,
there is a yearning, a longing, a calling out for help
to release the shackles of internalized hatred.

Moving through this world as a little black boy,
people rarely talk about your goodness.

Your rightness.
Your beauty.
Your brilliance.
And, your worthiness.

You are wanted.
You are loved.
You are needed.
And, you are good.

You are good.
You. Are. Good.

The pain we hide does not have to be your maker.
The pain can be a blip.
A brief period where you learned.
Grew.
Grieved.
And, rebooted.

As a young black boy, I masked my pain with smiles,
false hope, and positivity: fearing my tears, my grief,
and my woes would be perceived as weak.

Now, I know it was fear.
Of myself.
Of my power.
Of my grace.
Of my peace.
Of my clarity.
Of my compassion.

Your pain can be your medicine.
Your pain can be the elixir you need and have been looking for.
Your pain can help you find your way back home.

Home to your beauty.
Your love.
Your goodness.
Your wellbeing.
And, your rightness.

It is okay to be scared.
It is okay to feel uncomfortable.
It is okay to not know.

But know this:
the pain inside is your soul's gift
to you.
Your family.
Your community.
The world.

Sharing the pain aloud
sends ripples – medicine – to those like you and me.
Beautiful.
Brilliant.
Bold.
Black men.

I DON'T WANT TO BE HERE ANYMORE

by Reginald A. Howard

Men and mental health used to sound like an oxymoron. When I was growing up, people in my neighborhood would utter intolerant statements like "boys don't cry," or, "suck it up," or, my favorite, "stop acting like a little girl."

People commonly assumed girls experienced different emotions – and boys did not. When boys showed different emotions, I observed how their feelings were considered a sign of weakness to predators like bullies. But I do not agree we should dismiss our emotions.

My personal experience with depression began when I learned I would be a father to a son. My Dad was in and out of my life since I was two years old. When I found out I was going to parent a son, the anxiety really started to kick in. I did not have a job, I did not have a car, and I was living with my mother. I was emotionally and financially unprepared to be a father.

The prospect of fatherhood revealed many conflicting thoughts. I did not want to be a "deadbeat Dad" but I also did not want to be ill-equipped. Unfortunately, these disturbing realizations led me to my first suicide attempt.

I texted a few close friends and some family members. I was distraught, and wrote, *"take care of my son. I don't want to be here anymore."* Through His grace and His mercy, someone came and rescued me from the bridge I felt compelled to jump from. But their efforts, alone, could not solve any of the problems which brought me to that bridge in the first place.

Later that night, I attempted to end my life again. I took some pills from the medicine cabinet at home. I wanted something – anything – to numb the recurring pain inside. When I awakened, my Godmother was banging on the door; she was one of the people who received my text messages stating, *"take care of my son. I don't want to be here anymore."*

My Godmother lovingly grabbed me and took me to her house. I was on suicide watch there, with ample time for an honest, personal, self-assessment. I decided to actively research the field of mental health and find solutions to my problems. I was looking for what I know, now, is a safe space to freely talk about what I was going through emotionally and mentally.

I wanted to be at peace.

Establishing safe spaces outside of therapy can help a lot. Men talk openly about various issues at the barbershop, in the locker room, etc. They sometimes have periodic conversations about their emotions in those (specific) places, but they will switch the dialogue when it starts to get too deep. Normally, all these situations were not intentional – they happen by default.

There is a growing need for more safe spaces which are intentionally designed for men to honestly express their emotions. The National Alliance on Mental Illness (NAMI) does a great job with the different support groups they offer around the country. Men and women receive peer support longed for within all of us.

Today, I am proud to serve as the Community Outreach Coordinator for Black Men Heal, an online service offering men of color quality pro bono therapy by providers of color. The mission of Black Men Heal is to provide access to community resources, mental health treatment, and psycho education to men of color. Black Men Heal currently features Kings Corner, a weekly online support group. Kings Corner has become a virtual safe space for men around the world.

When I reflect on my personal journey with mental health, I remember the absence of safe spaces in my community, at home, or school. I believe the lack of education around the stigma associated with mental health played a role in my silence. I would not seek treatment for mental health until 2018 – well into my late 20's. I was labeled a demon child before I was born.

My family has a lineage of mental health history, yet only a few sought treatment due to the shame which accompanies mental health issues. My fears of being hurt, judged, and rejected impacted my personal growth. As such, I would continue to have multiple battles throughout my childhood: rarely saying anything to anyone.

Being an integral part of the NAMI Ending the Silence Team in Philadelphia is a blessing. In fact, young Black boys often come up to me expressing their innermost feelings. Does this happen because I was able to emotionally connect with the young Black men, or, does this happen because they (finally) had the opportunity to collectively experience a safe space provided for them to express themselves fully?

Honestly, I would say the latter. I recently had a conversation with my son on my podcast, Black Mental Health, regarding his emotions. I do not want my son to harbor feelings of alienation, isolation or separation – as if he does not have a safe space to express himself. If the stigma attached to mental health is not broken early, our youth may encounter tragic consequences.

Ironically, enduring multiple battles with mental health gave me courage, gratitude, and strength, but my experiences could have been fatal had I not sought treatment. I was clinically diagnosed with Major Depression Disorder and an unspecified case of anxiety. I am currently being monitored for Post-Traumatic Stress Disorder (PTSD) because of my recent car accident.

I share my experience with others because I am graced with the language to express myself instead of the impulse to hurt myself. I no longer feel ashamed to cry when I feel depressed. I no longer feel I ought to "suck it up" when I feel anxious. I no longer feel I "act like a girl" because I am scared to drive – a frightening symptom which accompanies living with PTSD.

Men and mental health does not sound like an oxymoron for me anymore. There are thousands of Black men across the globe who are honestly and openly talking about their emotional lives. I believe a man who chooses to challenge and confront the harsh realities of his mental health is truly the tough guy in my book.

WHEN EVERYBODY GOES HOME
by Josh Odam

The journeys of coming into one's Blackness and queerness are difficult ones. For Black men, like myself, who refuse to choose between them, we are faced with rejection, ostracization, and complete dismissal of our lived experiences.

We endure violence on an emotional, institutional, physical, and psychological level.

I vividly remember discussing the 1969 Stonewall Uprising as a college student. In discussing the legacy of police violence against protestors and demonstrators, my colleague, a white gay man, confidently asserted "gay has been and still is the new Black." Dumbfounded by his brazenness, I said, "what about the unique struggles of Black LGBTQ people?" He claimed my question was "divisive," and symbolic of the "infighting which slows down our movement."

After class, I spoke to a former mentor, a Black heterosexual man, to process what I heard. He smirked and said, "That gay stuff isn't for us anyway." Neither man knows I'm queer. Neither man was aware of the ways I was left without sanctuary in their individual spaces. I made a vow that day: my work and scholarship would be dedicated to creating and maintaining space for my Black queer body to exist wholly.

The Movement for Black Lives shifted the way folks conceptualize Black Liberation. I traveled to Ferguson, Missouri in August 2014 to participate in the Weekend of Resistance. I stood in the street where Michael Brown was fatally shot by a white male police officer – his Black body laid in the sun for several hours.

Protestors fighting for justice were met with heavily armored police vehicles and officers in military gear beating their batons against the sidewalk. Activists centered Blackness and queerness in their critique of state-sanctioned violence. This movement was founded and led by Black queer women, yet narratives were dominated by cisgender heterosexual Black men.

I heard men in the crowd shout homophobic and transphobic slurs at Black queer activists working to secure justice for Michael Brown's family. Some accused these activists of being agents sent to promote the "gay agenda." Their disdain and vitriol disturbed my soul. An organizer told me, "we are fighting for Black lives, too, but they don't care. The white gay community doesn't care. The straight Black people don't care. The police definitely don't care. We are targeted, but no one pays attention because they hate Black queer and Trans people that much."

When I returned to UMass, racist death threats were directed towards Black students. I witnessed various administrators, counselors, and faculty attempt to dismiss Black students' fears, instead of providing them with the resources they need to eradicate white supremacist behavior in our school. But one of my proudest moments occurred when the Center for Counseling and Psychological Health established a support group devoted to healing from racial trauma.

Despite the campus successes, I was hurting mentally and spiritually.

At the time, I believed conscious efforts towards self-care would harm the cause. Caring for myself was selfish, and the only meaningful contributions happened when I pushed myself to exhaustion. By default, I aggressively stifled and severed parts of my being deemed undesirable from the male gaze – the unsure parts, the softer parts, the queerer parts.

After deep reflection and intensive therapy, I realized my downward spiral was exacerbated by upholding rigid and restrictive standards of masculinity. Subconsciously, I embodied the coveted masculinity which I thought had long escaped me. However, when I was alone, I saw the myriad of ways in which my humanity was compromised.

I withdrew from school,

lost several meaningful relationships,

faced potential commitment into a psychiatric facility, and...

...attempted to take my own life.

During my recovery process, I was introduced to Lora Mathis' concept of "radical softness." Mathis, an introspective artist, musician, and poet, describes radical softness as "the idea that unapologetically sharing your emotions is a political move and a way to combat the societal idea that feelings are a sign of weakness. It is a tactic against a society which prioritizes a lack of emotions." When asked of radical softness is for everyone, Mathis responded:

"That doesn't feel fair for me to determine. I can't speak for everyone. I am a white, cis passing...and from an upper middle-class background. I have so many privileges that shape my perspective and experiences. I have been critiqued for this work and been told that it comes from a place of white privilege. And that's absolutely true. I am white, with white privilege, and this (despite my attempts to constantly undo it) influences my work."

I agree with Mathis' admission of her white privilege. Whiteness affords white people with an inherited and unearned safety to explore a softness many Black people will never access. However, I still believe Black queer men exploring radical softness is a worthy project for us to investigate.

My therapist recommended I read Sisters of the Yam: Black Women and Self-Recovery by bell hooks. I read testimonies of Black femmes engaging in personal and communal processes of healing from trauma. The book provides blueprints for shedding oppressive social constructs which impede authentic self-love. It was a sobering moment when I realized how few collective spaces exist for Black men to engage in similar practices.

Jack W. Sattel, in his article, The Inexpressive Male: Tragedy or Sexual Politics, puts forth several hypotheses as to why men do not delve into such vulnerable, expressive spaces with each other. He posits, "That, in itself, male inexpressiveness is of no particular value in our culture. Rather, it is an instrumental requisite for assuming adult male roles of power."[1]

Getting better meant relinquishing power – communally and personally. To truly heal, I had to shift the ways I engage and relate to other Black men in my circle and vice versa. This essay is only a small glimpse of the manner in which I lost and found myself several times over.

When I reflect on trauma I endured from anti-Blackness, queer antagonism, and hetero-patriarchal masculinity, I still deeply believe in our capacity for healing and growth as Black men.

My emotional journey altered my academic and professional trajectory. Black people deserve healing to cope with the stressors of repressive gender roles and our anti-Black world. The questions I am most interested in are: how do Black people heal when the structures designed to kill us are functioning? What must be confronted for Black men to see each other as confidants not competitors? How do we break the colonizers' grip to ensure all Black lives are centered? How do we hold each other while healing from trauma so the burden is not displaced on to our loved ones?

Most importantly, how do we heal ourselves, for ourselves?

---

[1] Sattel, The Inexpressiveness Male: Tragedy or Sexual Politics, 1976.

LIVING IN THE MAN BOX
by Mychal Sledge

When I was eight years old, I was playing in my room and heard my Mom scream, "Mychal!" I ran into the kitchen. She was preparing our food, but I saw her standing on a chair jumping up and down and screaming, "Mychal kill that mouse!"

I beat the mouse with a broom until he stopped moving. She hugged and thanked me. My Dad was at work and we were home alone. I never told my mother I was fearful of mice and wanted to scream and stand on the kitchen chair with her. I was traumatized.

Another traumatic event in my life also included my mother. I came home crying because some boys down the block took my bike. She told me, "Go back downstairs, get your bike and don't come back until you have it." But I worried those kids were older and could fight.

My reality quickly shifted. I was thrusted into the "man box." I went downstairs, fought those boys, and got my bike. Later, my mother said, "Never let anyone take anything from you and never let them see you cry." I learned how to fight scared, never let anyone take anything from me - and **never cry**.

Unknowingly, the man box shaped my spiritual journey.

I learned my personal mental health is deeply rooted. I can recall what I fed my young mind and psyche. I envisioned what a father and head of the household does, which I embraced; many of my friends did not share my beliefs about manhood. I was taught a man prays daily. A man is gentle, kind and loving. A man works hard and provides for his family.

The story in my family is he married my mother when I was one year old. I believed I was raised by my father. However, one of my cousins shared the first of many family secrets. I asked my mother and she responded, "I thought you knew." Afterwards, she did something I never witnessed and would never see again. I saw her cry.

A few years later she introduced me to my biological father. He lived in Brooklyn. We lived in Harlem. That same day I created a relationship with my grandmother. My father did not talk much. In fact, he spent most of the day quietly observing as his mother loved on me. Despite her best efforts, I was full of rage yet did not know why. **I could not handle my emotions.**

The only father I knew enrolled me in the Martial arts when I was 110. I had no siblings. I cultivated an insatiable passion for the Martial arts. I excelled in Karate School. I started to compete in tournaments. I lost often. I sparred with older kids who beat me, and I could not cry. These difficult moments ultimately fueled my desire to win.

I was awarded Black Belt in two different Martial arts systems by age 15.

One of the valuable principles we learned in Karate School was practicing Zen Meditation. I saw the face of my biological father when my mind was quiet. After one year of Zen Meditation, I began to win every spar I competed in school. I started winning fights – beating the exact same competitors I once lost to.

Still, **I never told anyone I was hurting** because I was not raised by my biological father. I was angry with my mother for betraying me with her dishonesty. The man I called Dad was not my real father. My troubled mind created a recurring theme: if my mother lied to me, how can I trust another woman?

My anger manifested in the ring; everyone saw the effects. My anger bothered me in specific ways. I had a familiar pattern of reactions - anger, madness, and rage. I had the same results: rage, self-destructive behavior, and verbal abuse. I was dangerous when my rage blinded me.

It was impossible to enjoy a happy relationship with anyone when I was angry.

No one asked me how I beat grown men when I was just 16. No one asked me why I behaved the way I did. Nonetheless, I became a national and international champion in Martial arts on five different occasions. I won two gold medals in the Pan-American Games. I competed in the open weight class and weight class. I was in the World Almanac five consecutive years.

But I never told anyone (how or why) I visualized my biological father each time I stepped in the ring. I fought him in every ring around the world. It did not matter whether I was competing in France, Japan or South America. His face was my toughest opponent,

Most of the women in my life had a favorite phrase for me: "get out!" I was trapped in a body and controlled by a mind which did not give a damn. I held on to childhood hurts, lies from my mother; those unaccepted truths were the source of my bondage. The pain seemed worse than a life bid in a maximum-security prison.

I could no longer blame everything on the 'systemic destruction of the Black Man,' or the Willie Lynch concepts. I had to release the fears, limitations and projections other people imposed upon me. I had to change my belief system. A friend once said, "Your opinion of me is not my reality." I believed him. I try and instill healthy beliefs with others. I am no longer sleeping at the light switch. I am no longer comfortable in the dark. I am no longer consciously dead. I will not accept the reality I am told. I will create the reality I need to fulfill purpose in my life.

I started therapy, and initially went because of my arguments or behavior at work. I worked for the federal government. I did not want to go to therapy but was mandated – if not I would lose my job. I thought my therapy sessions would be exactly like what I saw on television shows and decided I was not going to lay on someone's couch because it would be a waste of my time.

I rejected someone's help before I accepted someone's help.

My first therapy session was in downtown Manhattan near Central Park. A white male greeted me at the door and invited me into his office. I saw no couch, and told myself, "He's not a real therapist." I discredited him immediately. Our sessions were framed by my fears. When he asked about my intentions, my job or myself, I would angrily respond and often say, "No!"

One day, after many non-productive sessions, my therapist asked, "Why are you always on the battlefield?" His question baffled, confused – and intrigued me. I said, "What?" He said, "Every time you come here you have on your army boots. You have on a helmet and army gear." I realized he wanted to understand the root of my anger. I laughed and said, "I am angry because you want me to lay on your couch." He said, "Look around. I do not even have a couch."

I later discovered the symbolic meaning of laying on a couch. I feared being exposed and vulnerable – especially with another man. I was uncomfortable with the idea of shedding the layers of my defense mechanisms. But I extended my sessions, to everyone's surprise. This was my first spiritual awakening in the process of understanding my spiritual journey.

Therapy helped me to uncover the paradox of how the Martial arts channeled my anger in a constructive manner. Partnering with my therapist helped change my perception of manhood: I was blessed with two fathers, and not just one who cared for me. I learned to empathize with challenges my mother faced because of her youthful inexperience as a parent. I acknowledged hate I carried for many years towards other people, and myself.

Our therapy sessions empowered me. I learned the value in forgiving other people, and most importantly, forgiving myself. I began to feel a sense of freedom. I learned to admit and share my feelings in a healthy manner is a natural part of my healing process. Ironically, the same person I judged and viewed with suspicion helped me accept the man God intended me to be.

As a child I was taught to conceal my vulnerability. My anger was a mask for confusion, fear and shame. My level of self-acceptance was inspired my level of self-awareness. My life began to change. I received promotions at work. I sustained committed relationships. I pray and meditate daily. I found a new understanding for my relationship with God, my brothers, my sisters and my community. I embody spiritual peace within. Today, I am God's humble servant.

I learned trauma was not my fault. Trauma was inflicted upon me due to other people's choices and experiences. I learned to let go of pain which does not serve me. I learned healing is my personal responsibility. I leaned my spiritual journey is a lifelong process. I learned the solution to mental suffering is spiritual nature because the suffering is spiritual in nature.

God inspired me to start a community-based nonprofit over two decades ago. The Sledge Group, Inc. is a 501 (c) (3) organization. We are one of the longest active mentoring and tutoring programs in Harlem for boys and girls, ages 13 to 18. We are dedicated to empowering our youth through education, and life experiences. We also provide free parent support groups.

"Service is the rent we pay for our room here on Earth." – Muhammad Ali

MANHOOD, MENTAL HEALTH AND MORE
by Ulrick J. Accime

My name is Ulrick J. Accime. I'm a Licensed Clinical Social Worker (LCSW) in Fort Lauderdale, Florida. I've been working in the mental health field for over five years. A large number of my clients are Black men. I also work with adolescents and adults. Our mental health healthy facility welcomes a diverse group of people, and we service people raised throughout the African Diaspora. Working with men from the Motherland is especially challenging: some mental health issues are unique to their culture, family and religion.

It is an honor and a privilege to partner with Black men who desire emotional independence, meaningful change and purposeful living. My clients are profoundly trapped by intergenerational trauma. Secrets and lies are passed down from one decade to the next. Many Black men have internalized negative messages by caretakers, dogma, society, teachers, etc. They were always told who they should be, and when they failed to meet others' standards, they felt they were less of a man.

Everyone seems to describe their families as dysfunctional. For some, their families are considered to be nightmares. A Black man in a broken home often adapts to the language of abuse in a way they perceive is normal. Many Black men admit being told not to lose a fight because "they would get their asses beat by their parents." Some Black men cope by expressing aggressive behavior. They were taught survival, not solutions. And, if they wanted something, they had to fight or take it from another person.

I treat Black men who sense estranged, indifferent and unloving relationships with their fathers is at the root of their troubles. These men have been looking for someone "real" most of their lives. They were not taught what it takes to be a father in a household. When faced with the responsibility of being a father, most repeat the cycle. Most don't accept their roles. Others run away. Some men abandon or reject fatherhood because they fear exposing their kids to the same mistreatment they received.

I have worked with survivors of sexual abuse. A large number of sexual assaults go unreported because of the stigma it holds for the survivors;

even more so for Black men. Some of my clients question their sexuality (and manhood) as a result of early childhood sexual abuse. Unresolved trauma can affect relationships with significant others. Some Black men, without adequate coping skills, harbor self-hatred. Some Black men cope with misguided anger, substance abuse and unhealthy relationships. Some Black men indulge in anonymous sexual encounters because their bodies don't matter to them.

Black men today are challenged by their overall mental health. Can you imagine how it feels to live in a society where you don't feel safe to express your emotions? Black men have been in a constant state of surveillance – inside and outside of their homes. A person's mind is damaged when you pump them daily with stress hormones similar to soldiers on the battlefield.

My clients often state they can neither enjoy their lives nor remember when they were happy. In fact, there's little to no time for joy when you're trying to keep yourself alive by any means necessary. Some of these men have been taught their lives are short and meaningless. Some drink alcohol and smoke weed regularly to self-medicate. But when the alcohol and weed stop working, they use harder drugs.

Black men have often been exposed to certain traumas which usually takes many, many years to heal from and recover. Some Black men learn they must be honest with themselves in order to let go of hurt, pain and suffering. The mask they wear is killing them in various ways. Black men who overcame adversity had to admit they had a problem and wanted help. They stopped running away from their issues and faced them head-on. Honest self-assessment is one of the keys to living in the solution. It's difficult to cultivate self-acceptance when you're always told who you should be – and you believe it.

From my perspective, I believe therapy is 100% effective for men recovering from trauma and other injustices. The right support from (just) one person can make a lasting difference. Counselors, family members, friends, mentors, professors, public servants and teachers can positively impact others. Every one of my clients who changed their lives for the better always mentioned the value of someone who believed in them.

I always encourage Black men to make gradual changes for themselves. They genuinely appreciate someone cheering them on and being in their corner. When they put all of their efforts into pleasing other people, it usually leads to disappointment. Another important tool is being realistic with their goals. I've noticed most of the success stories come from men who take small steps one day at a time.

Black boys need the love and safety all children deserve. When you're always told and shown the world is afraid of you, it hurts what you believe and how you feel about yourself. Black men need to be taught new coping skills with culturally competent caregivers. Black men ought to unlearn old ideas of brokenness, helplessness and worthlessness. Black men are capable enough to learn from their past mistakes. They are unique human beings and have a life worth living. I want them to know that!

ONCE UPON A TIME, I WAS WEAK
by Steven G. Fullwood

I hate the word, weak.

"Weak" epitomizes everything I wished to escape. Weak means someone else has control, someone else runs my life. Weak means they were able to get into my consciousness, under my radar and break me down. Weak means it happened because I was not strong enough to handle it. Weak means I cannot be who I am. Weak is not what I am. I am not weak.

When I was a child, I was called smart; a genius, but my mind felt weak. Soon understand genius is something you produce – not something you are. Could not focus on my work in class, could not read each sentence, often made mistakes, did not know, did not know.

Weak.

In the second grade, I was sent to the principal's office. I was told to pick out a new shirt from a big box of clothing. I chose a yellow plaid shirt. Thought I was lucky. But it was only because the shirt I had on was ripped in different places and hanging off my small body.

Weak became my identity when I was a child. A weakling. Not strong. Skinny as all get out. Could not prevent a flying fist in my eye, my stomach, and my chest. Punched. Slapped. Beaten.

Weak.

One day I knocked down a rough boy in my neighborhood. I had no upper body strength to keep him down. He pushed me off him easily, got up, laughed, and took all the cook kids with him, leaving me alone.

And weak.

Witnessed my mother endure emotional and physical abuse. She, too, was weak. She said she was going to leave him. Leave him. Please. Yes, one day he'd look up and she'd be gone, she said. Leave him. Leave him. A mantra.

Some glorious, non-abusive life waited for us all, behind the front door. For momma, my four siblings and me. We went slammed against the door, but not through it. Instead, momma cried, hollered, laughed, read, sat, slept – and worked. Momma stayed.

He stayed, too. Father strong, not weak. Angry. Big. Imposing. Why so damn angry? So not weak. Caught me dancing in the living room early one morning to "Mighty Real" by Sylvester. Told me he knew all about me. Shook his head. What did he know? He knew I was weak. A faggot. What would he do?

My second-hand clothes were already thin. Wore them till they fell off my body. Shared clothes with brother. Not enough to go around, we had to share. Given excuses. Why can I not have money, new clothes, new something other than old this. This.

Had no balls, literally. Have one testicle. Did not know boys were supposed to have two until high school. Not totally true. Knew my brother had two. But I had one. Born defective.

"Feminine. Faggot. Punk. Sissy. A little sugar in his tank. Watch that one. Stop acting like a girl. You act like a girl. Stop it!" Daily litany. Worse as the years wore on. All I could do is run. Run. And hide. I learned how to hide, be with my self, be strong – not at the mercy of others. A friend could easily be a foe.

Winter in Toledo. Cold in our house. Cold in my bedroom. Cold air punching at the plastic over the winter window, punching at my stomach, grabbing at my throat. No sleep. Cold water to wash up in. cold walk to school. Cold.

Teenager. Sex drive high. Jacked off several times a day to...anything. Jacked to sister's *Playgirl* carefully returning afterward to her room the way I found it. First orgasm. Second orgasm. Millions of orgasms. Voyeur. Across the alley I watched a man undress almost every night. Late at night my eyes flied open to gaze at the only thing I wanted to see: a naked man. I could not help myself.

Graduated high school. Big deal. What now? Worked at Pizza Hut. Uncomfortable around white people. Didn't want or understand their Black questions. Did not want them to find out I was born poor, lived poor, did not know some things, so many things. Stupid.

Joined the Army. A chance to become strong. During the physical exam, standing among two dozen naked men, the doctor feels me up, asks me to cough. Sent me to another room with four others. Told my left testicle or right one did not descend, is still stuck in me, likely cancerous. Get operation, he said. Come back. Back? Sent home on a long bus ride. Paralyzed.

Go to hospital. Operation will get it, the man part. It did not descend, is removed. Felt better, felt worse. At least I had it in me. At least there are two. Asked the doctor/nurse/whoever could it be placed in my ball sac. She said no. Assured me I could still father children. Kids?

Faggot revisited. At 20, began having sex with known Faggot. Faggot here now. Faggot blows me. Then my cover. Okay, I am. Am what? Gay? Bisexual? I am I do not know. Weak. Cannot make a decision. Roll with being gay. Homosexual.

Try to build a house with this idea. Idea implodes. All my dreams contain locker rooms, naked men, being on stage and being violated. Become Faggot. Faggot hiding. I like men. I love them. I crave them. I need them. Am not one, so I need to replace me with one.

Began college. Cannot focus in class. My clothes are...my mind is... my face, my face...My hair is unruly. Cannot help it. I don't care. What am I doing here? I am not smart. I do not deserve to be here. On probation at school. Take next quarter off.

Rejected by someone I loved. Broken, destroyed, humiliated, spent; a mass of jelly in skin. Walked to Emergency Room at hospital several blocks from my apartment. Told them through bawling I want to commit suicide. Sent elsewhere. Admitted to mental institution for observation. Slept on a cot for two days across from a dirty, crazy white boy. Crazy people stayed there.

All I wanted is someone to hear me, love me. Please. Convinced doctor I am okay. Crazy black boy is fine now, so let me go, let me out of here. Left after two days of suicide watch on my accord. Walked home. The sun shined. Tired of pain I reveal to anyone. Throat packed. Afraid to be alone.

Became expert at quickies. Fuck brothers like me. Pick them up and take them back to my apartment. Convince myself no one understands me, except these men and they are mute. They are weak. They are me.

The first man I dated was 22 years older than me. He has a job, so I go out with him because he asked. I was lonely. He says it has been 10 years, he is not HIV-positive. Let him fuck me without a condom. I resist inside. He came inside me. Often. I test negative, repeatedly, always terrified.

After leaving him, I dated a married man. His wife knew about him, maybe us. Why does she stay with him, I rationalized? Married Man and I met at our secret love-nest. One night, his other male lover stopped by. They fought outside. There is blood between them.

My married lover took off in his car. His lover returned to the love-nest, where I sat shaking and threw a bloody handkerchief in my face. Took me two hours to get home on foot. Exhausted. Lied in bed staring at my ceiling.

And.

These stories happened over 30 years ago. I wrote them down over 20 years ago. Sharing them with you is cathartic. These stories cease to be mine. By reading them, like all stories, they become yours.

Stories are amorphous, ongoing, ever-changing; an adventure. They refuse to be simple or simplified. This heart in many ways healed because I wrote them down, honoring them. I do not think I could have arrived here without going there, places of unimaginable pain and misery.

And, there is more here than I could have seen back then. A lot of joy and pleasure obscured by trauma. I needed to tell these stories, but not only because of feeling devastated: I thought I experienced all this pain and echo for nothing. And I could not have that.

The original essay, "Weak," unexamined, reduces me to who and what I thought I was based on definitions of life I did not consciously choose, or in many ways, agree with. It is an essay if you took it and threw it to the ground; other stories would spider out onto your feet.

Beautiful, amazing, cosmic stories next to and sometimes hovering above the painful ones. I grew up in a house where my mother was abused, yes, but she was not the sum of her abuse, not at all. Neither am I. Nor am I even the sum of my own thoughts and impressions. Neither are you.

"Weak" is now your story. Which, I think, is a good thing. "Weak" offers you entry into my lived experiences. But if you are truly lucky it will shed light on your own stories. And that is all we have, really, each other and our stories.

LONDON TOWN: THE SECRET LIFE OF A TOP BOY
by Ronald Dodzro

As a young Black man growing up in Wandsworth (South West London England), I was accustomed to and affiliated with gang life. ABM, Brown Gang, 031, SUK, and TZ are local gangs which shaped my childhood experience. However, as most young Black men know, the lure of multiple gangs in close range brings animosity, danger and violence.

Gang-involved young adults increase their risk of violence as perpetrators, victims and witnesses – something I know firsthand. A UK study found 90% of male gang members (aged 18-34) were involved in violence in the past five years; 80% of male gang members reported at least three violent incidents **(Cold et al., 2013).**

Racist media outlets normally reference "Black on Black" crime as indicative of culturally induced evil fatality or violent injury. However, one aspect often omitted is the trauma experienced by young Black men **(Cuff & Matheson, 2015)**. Trauma developed from painful events Black men experience and/or witness may precipitate Post Traumatic Stress Disorder (PTSD) symptomology.

PTSD is an anxiety disorder which occurs following exposure to an extremely catastrophic or threatening event, like severe violence. Individuals may re-experience trauma, avoid stimuli associated with the trauma and will have increased arousal. Trauma can lead to difficulty concentrating, irritability, outbursts of anger or trouble sleeping peacefully.

Additionally, people may endure flashbacks and nightmares. Traumatic experiences lead to altered perceptions of safety in daily life, causing people to remain in a heightened state of panic and threat **(Overstreet & Braun, 2000)**. High levels of PTSD are linked to violent experiences, and the more violence a young person is exposed to the greater the PTSD symptoms **(Abram et al., 2004).**

Research examining trauma among Black men shows about 62% directly experienced a traumatic event in their lifetime, 72% witnessed a traumatic event, and 59% learned of a traumatic event involving a family member or friend **(Motley & Banks, 2018)**. Many young Black men are burdened with trauma and I see their heavy shoulders. Exposure to trauma is unfortunately a daily reality for many young Black men **(Bertram & Dartt, 2008)**.

One of the biggest factors preventing young Black men from accessing support, in my observation, is "toxic masculinity" combined with a "street code." These default social constructs and norms lead to informal rules which govern their response to situations in a public setting. Young Black men are expected to "man up" or they "need to stop being a pussy." But they lack coping skills to deal with the emotional ramifications of trauma.

Some young Black men have internalized cultural beliefs about engaging with therapeutic interventions. As such, their actions constitute "snitching" if they disclose pertinent details about traumatic events. Their perceived conflicts with the street code sometimes create anxiety. Young Black men who experience or witness a traumatic event do not rely on the police if they fear confrontation or threatened. The street code demands they must handle these situations themselves if they face such problems.

In my personal and professional life, I see young Black men struggling to acknowledge or cope with PTSD symptoms and trauma. As a result of not knowing how to respond, they normally react in the following ways:

- Some will self-medicate with alcohol or drugs. It is common for young Black men to use cannabis to help numb their feelings and symptoms; there is a destructive relationship between substance abuse, trauma and violent injuries.

- Some will isolate and withdraw into their homes, avoiding people and the streets.

- Some will escape their residential areas, or live with other family members, hoping to appease their feelings of anxiety.

- Some will not have this luxury and will be forced to remain in their environment, and relive constant traumatic moments. They may also face possible retaliation of serious injury - or death. People will arm themselves or recruit friends to exact revenge **(Rich & Grey, 2005)**. *("They took an L but made sure the next letter coming was M." Ghetts – Window Pain).*

What is being done for young Black men today? Who helped my my family, friends and acquaintances when they were caught up within violent traumatic events? Black men are approximately half as likely as their white counterparts to use professional mental health services **(Hankerson et al., 2011)**. I anticipate this statistic to get worse when we focus on young Black men and trauma.

Due to the prevalence of trauma among this group, we need to do better as a community to ensure their needs are being met. How are we providing a safe space for young Black men to discuss their traumas? *("Torn between seeing a therapist or a pastor, think about it, heaven or hell, what would you rather? I've lost friends I still hope to see in this life after."* - Chip – 0420 (R.I.P. Black the Ripper). How are they coping with what they have seen and done? *("How can I talk about killing my opps and in the same breath say Black Lives Matter? My issues are deep rooted."* Ghetts – Mad About Bars S5: E7).

What provisions are in place for young Black men to access support from Black mental health professionals like myself? Who are the Black male professionals which can identify with and understand the intricacies to get people entangled within gang life and violence? Many of those who experience or witness traumatic events will be forced to continue behaving as if nothing happened – they will return to their communities with no support.

Interventions need to be developed to establish a sense of manhood, safety, self-esteem, and strength in these young Black men. Historically, they rarely access support from mental health services after a traumatic event. However, effective treatment and psycho education could address the common and harmful behaviors they adopted (carrying weapons and substance abuse, i.e.).

As a Cognitive Behavioral Therapist (CBT), I know trauma-focused interventions help alleviate PTSD symptoms. These interventions help manage anxiety and modify maladaptive cognitions related to traumatic events. Clients are taught relaxation skills, coping strategies and how to manage their emotions before trauma-specific components are addressed **(Cohen, Berliner & Mannarino, 2010)**.

Bronfenbrenner's ecological theory is a psychological concept I believe can help young Black men at a systemic level. This theory explains how an individual is located within a nested structure of "systems" and further states how an individual is influenced by their social context and relationships with others such as family, friends and institutional systems. As brothers and sisters within the Black community, we need to be cognizant of these "systems" to better help facilitate progressive change for young Black men.

At the macro system level, we need legislation and policies created to foster mental health care, specifically focusing on the adverse outcomes and traumatic experiences of young Black men. We need culturally competent psychologists. We need to build young Black men's resilience. We need to involve the Black community in service development. We need to make cultural adaptations within interventions to make them more relatable to this population **(Lindsay, Strand & Davis, 2011)**.

The voices of young Black men suffering with trauma need to be heard. Their personal stories can help deepen our compassion, empathy and understanding as a collective of how they feel after experiencing or witnessing a traumatic event. The UK rap scene affirms their pain and redemption, which is why I respect artists such as Chip, and Ghetts.

People within our community and mainstream society are quick to criminalize and marginalize young Black men, but neither comprehend nor understand the vicious webs they are trapped within. As a young Black man our souls are wounded and we need to heal before this cycle of trauma continues and is inherited by the next generation.

I have known young Black men who are perpetrators, victims and witnesses of traumatic events such as gun crime and knife crime. I do not see these men as "less than." I believe we live in an unequal society with racial injustice.

Some young Black men learned how to adjust in society and make life easier. But society has dehumanized young Black men. Instead of using community and psychological approaches we know exist, we neglect them when they do wrong. I believe we need to explore how we, as individuals, can improve their health and well-being and think about the varying levels of possible intervention. We ALL have a responsibility to provide the nurturing and support lacking in the lives of our young Black men.

MY JOURNEY WITH MENTAL ILLNESS
by Alvin Smith

Mental illness among Black men is a delicate topic. Whose culture are we supposed to emulate? Some of us do not know our own traditions. We were stripped of our culture. How should we act? The margin of sanity is beyond our control. We are not viewed as full beings: slave masters saw us as 3/5 human.

Black men are dehumanized by American laws. Whose standards are the example of how we should think and behave? If we speak "proper," they will say "he is trying to be white." Go within Black man. Get in touch with your instincts and humanity to know what to do about these contradictions.

We are told directly, and in these times, symbolically, we are inferior to white men. We had to believe it to survive in the past. There was no time to question sanity. Our existence is decided by people who did not have our best interest. Lies and myths are passed on from our forefathers through each generation.

I was not a problem academically. My behavior caused trouble. I could not do the right thing in class. I got into fights often; sometimes the class bully, other times it was racially motivated, especially in all-white parochial schools. I was called a nigger – and fought back. Teachers embarrassed me in front of students. I was outnumbered. After numerous suspensions I was expelled – from seven different Catholic schools.

I lived with my grandfather. He had good intentions for me, but did not know the humiliation I endured in class. He would not hear my side of the story. He felt the nuns were always right. He wanted me to have the best education yet often sided with them: against me. I believed there was something "wrong" with me, but my spirit knew it was the system of oppression.

My grandfather is from Haiti. He knew hardship. He came to America to find opportunity, and he did. He worked as a security guard for Jamel Mansion. His intentions were to provide me a good education by sending me to Catholic School. He prepared me to become a white-collar worker. But corporate jobs did not work out because my skills were conductive to the arts.

I excelled at writing. I won the spelling bee every year. The school psychiatrist said I had Attention Deficit Disorder (ADD). During my sessions with doctors they watched me play with Cowboys and Indians. I purposely did not make them fight. In my adventures, the Indians negotiated getting their land back. Soon, they had to fight. I made the Indians win. I empathized with Indigenous people. As such, my fighting was purposeful.

The last parochial school I got kicked out of was Rice High School. I was expelled but they were mistaken. Someone robbed the coat check at the high school dance. My friends and I were falsely accused of stealing. My grandfather was furious with me. He could not see the oppression I was experiencing. Again, I was judged wrongfully. Still, my grandfather agreed with the school. He believed you should take advantage of an opportunity to get ahead in life. His beliefs were not wrong, but certain schools were not right for me.

No matter how I tried otherwise, I would end up fighting students who sought to humiliate me in front of the class. I refused to accept their behavior. I fought back no matter the cost. After leaving Rice, an all-boys school, I went to the High School of the Humanities, downtown in Greenwich Village. I wanted to go to LaGuardia, a high school for the arts, but my grandfather did not see the purpose of art in my life.

I was happy at Humanities. I made lots of friends. It was a multi-cultural school. My friends came from various nationalities, which helped me. I became emerged in the sub-culture of the punk rock scene downtown. My friends and I hung out in the Lower East Side. The punk world fit perfectly with my personality. The names of the bands encapsulated my life experiences. I could identify with groups like The Ejected, The Expelled and The Exploited.

I remained a part of the punk rock scene for three years until I dropped out of high school in the 11th grade, which was a mistake. Later, I fell in love with a girl from my Harlem neighborhood. It was not my intention to leave school, but I wanted to live on my own. I am grateful, though, because I found a comfortable social life at the High School of the Humanities: I finally fit in!

April was attractive. I liked her apartment. I moved in with her. I had no money, but we made ends meet with our telemarketing jobs. We lived together for two years, and then it fell apart. I was in my mid 20's, and went to live with my grandfather again. April moved across the street. I would see her coming home from school in the afternoon sometimes, but we did not talk.

I was diagnosed with Bipolar Disorder in my early 30's. I started hearing voices. I believed these voices were a spirit trying to lead me somewhere. The voices said get out of the house. I was frantic and would leave in search of whatever the voices said. I heard voices regularly and I would listen. It made sense to listen. But my life became increasingly more difficult. My family thought my behavior was insane.

As a result of these frightening episodes, I was hospitalized several times. The voices stopped and later resurfaced. My grandfather did not understand my erratic behavior and kicked me out. I lived with family members periodically, but the recurring voices led to my uncontrollable actions. Some people were scared to be in my presence. And, I was homeless.

I was homeless five years, alternating between various residences, shelters, and squats. Despite my daily challenges, I became a noted spoken word artist. Poetry gave my life clarity, meaning and perspective. I thrived at Open Mic nights, performing at celebrated venues such as the Brooklyn Moon Café, Joe's Public Theater and Nuyorican Poets Café.

My aunt signed me up to live at a residency in Hell's Kitchen. The facility got me off the streets, but I still could not do some of the things I wanted to do with my life. Although I valued my experiences doing spoken word, I felt like I was holding on to a safe, creative past. I wrote a play, Raw Materials, directed by Gregory Gates, co-founder of Imagenation Cinema. Gates later arranged a meeting with a writer at the New York Times. Gregory became a trusted mentor.

The writer intended to publish an article about my play, and document my personal journey as well. I was excited; this opportunity could impact my future. But the writer needed permission from the residency, and they rejected his wishes, stating the project was *"too high functioning... we're just concentrating on his recovery at this point."*

I was so hurt. I left the residency in six months. I moved to the Bronx and lived with some family members, but did not feel comfortable doing my art there. I went back to the streets. I became my own payee for my disability checks. I slept at friends' houses, by the highway, or in squats.

I survived one day at a time.

Eventually, I went to a drop-in center on Bowery Street. I lived there for six months and got a bed in the Bowery Residents' Committee (BRC). I lived in that shelter for one year. Afterwards, I moved into a supportive housing residence which offered more flexibility. I lived there for over two years. Later, I moved to a place in the Bronx, where I now reside.

Black men are stigmatized for living with mental illness. Black men are unjustly perceived as criminal threats in our racist society. Black men sometimes misplace their anger – we do not feel sick physically, but doctors often tell us we are sick. Mania is a symptom of mental illness. There were consecutive days when I was unable to sleep.

When I am in a manic state, it is (now) understandable something is not right. Similarly, hearing voices is a symptom of mental illness. Depression is another symptom of mental illness. It can be helpful to ask yourself: what am I depressed about? Part of my depression was rooted in not getting my basic human needs met: adequate shelter, creative expression, decent food, i.e.

My unpredictable behavior would show up with other people unannounced. Also, it is common for people to hear the voice of the subconscious mind and the voice of temptation. It is part of the human struggle to distinguish these voices. My behavior did not make sense until I stopped harming myself.

I believe God tested my faith by putting me in a situation to question my sanity, and to seek out healthy ways of sane living. If I start thinking of a way to make these voices tell me about the future or think of it as a supernatural power, I am being grandiose and selfish. Furthermore, the ego will confuse you and make you believe you are deeper than the rest of humanity.

I have endured a spiritual battle, not just a mental illness. I pay attention to my thinking and make sure it does not lead me to extremes. I went back to school and humbly earned my G.E.D. Through grace and mercy, I have some measure of stability in my life. I am grateful for the simple pleasures, small victories and successful days. I have more clarity and less symptoms.

THE POWER OF BEING – A PATH TO THRIVING
by Brandon Bolden

It is impossible to be a Black man without facing judgment.

Being a Black man is paradoxical in nature. Our gender can wield us power, but our ethnicity and race simultaneously can strip it away. The success of the Black man can wage war. The failures of the Black man's efforts can yield it backlash.

It is remarkable how the pain of judgment impacts the lives of Black men. The pain of judgment shows up through addiction, instability, self-harm, self-hatred, trauma and violence. Even in the most gifted among us, the pain of judgment shows up.

Judgment can impede the lives of Black men with great dread, exacerbating the struggle with who we believe ourselves to be. Judgment invites avoidance and denial. Judgment encourages us to chase meaningless endeavors and hide our emotions. Judgments stunts our ability to perform and wreaks havoc on our personal development. As such, we might show up wearing the projections of the world rather than visions of our moral compass.

Some truths, by default, create well-known, Black male narratives. But with the power of judgment seemingly against us, how do we, as Black men, in our society thrive? "Just be you," was the answer my older brother gave me when I asked him a similar question while playing a one-on-one game of basketball. He said, "You got something special, but everybody does not want that special something you got."

My older brother gave me wisdom. He transformed from being a loyal gang member to a community role model. I watched him alter his mannerisms and model how he treated other people. I witnessed his morals change as he encountered various truths about who he believed himself to be.

Each shift my brother made came with judgment. Despite his transformation he was harshly criticized. Some people never grew to trust his evolution. His criminal past denied him many opportunities. My brother endured dark days and regrets; his life was perfect. Still, he was determined to persevere and let nothing stop him from being who he believed himself to be.

"...Oh, and don't feel like you have to be a superman all the time. You can be a student, too," he calmly remarked after making a game-winning, step back three-point shot (he obviously studied my footwork because I did not see it coming).

My brother learned from various mentors, public figures and role models what it means to be authentically human. My brother convinced others they were safe with his attention to detail and disarmed you with his goofy jokes. Even when treated unjustly he changed the narrative with his kindness and selflessness – values he internalized from observing world leaders and other affirming examples around him.

As his awareness shifted, his environment, too, had to shift. It was remarkable how exercising his power to be his authentic self unconsciously gave others permission to do the same. His transformation allowed him to let go of some old patterns, which caused many people to forget his past unless it was brought up in their interactions.

Ultimately, my brother was a man who became respected by other people, instead of being feared by other people. He was regarded as a giver and not a taker. I did not realize until recently he shared with me how the power of healing within can have on the self and others, even though some folks' criticism never ceased.

His insights helped me accept the world has always judged Black men. He warned me not to let those judgments discourage us from being free. In fact, in this society, human beings are programmed to judge; it is a part of how we survive in a world full of current and generational threats to our unique identity as Black men.

My brother reminded me judgments are not useful, especially if they do not serve us in the here and now. I believe if he allowed the judgments connected to his past to compromise his present thoughts, feelings and behaviors, his newfound humility would not be so attractive to other people.

Sometimes we forget we have a say in who we are. Sometimes we forget we can choose how to respond to the internal forces and external voices. Affirming our humanity can give us opportunities to go beyond perceived limitations. We embody feminine and masculine energy. We can possess finesse and power. We can think creatively and logically. Our identities do not have to be bland, dichotomous and straight-edged. We can expand as deep and wide as our imagination and willpower.

Allowing ourselves to be, and using judgment to our advantage, can be powerful - which seems too good to be true. My brother's life is a testament for unlimited possibility. His legacy was formed by thriving in narratives he chose. He let go of the demons and dishonor of his past. He was motivated to grow. He did not force himself to be anything beyond his truth in the present moment. He did not have to settle for being another Obama or Tupac: he could just be himself.

In March of 2016, my brother was in the middle of an altercation with the intention of de-escalating potential harm. My brother sought to resolve conflict through peaceful actions – something he now valued – instead of violence, which he was accustomed to in the past.

Despite his efforts, he was shot and killed.

One member involved was unwilling to reconcile the situation. Many of my brother's friends learned about his evolution during his funeral. They were impacted by the senseless loss and the new life my brother shined from the darkness. His example inspired some to re-evaluate their lives and their purpose to society. Many surrendered the gang life and began to discover their value as Black men.

And, like my brother, some gang members became leaders in their communities.

Black men thrive when we commit to discovering and being our authentic, full and unique selves. We learn we have the power to respond to judgment. Black men thrive when we understand not all judgments are useful, even those from seemingly trustworthy sources like our families, friends and people in authority. Black men thrive when we own the autonomy to choose who we are, and who we are not, through accepting the complexity, discernment and wonder of our human fallibility. Black men thrive when caring for their mental health.

Black men must welcome the grace of curiosity; we should explore our uniqueness and learn how to courageously express and harness this energy. Black men ought not to feel guilt and shame for being. Clarity and healing occur as we give ourselves permission to be.

Judgment can become a tool of empowerment which informs us, rather than a weapon for self-destruction, on our journey of thriving with mental health. I believe my brother would be proud to know today Black men have more opportunities to experience the gift of being, despite the pain of judgment.

PAIN - ANGER - JOY

by Devan Dmarcus

Pain.

Why do I feel
so much of you?

You make me
insane
and I feel like
touching you
out of
Anger.

Because you manipulated
my angel
into walking away
with you
to that place where
Joy
was found.

But not for me
because
now my hands
and knees
are to the
cold ground

and pain jolts
through my body
and I have
no medicine
that can aid
in stopping

the everlasting
Anger I feel
towards so many
of my peers
whom
inevitably
will
end up dead with
Joy...

Hopefully
the man
will get to see
his little boy
before
he leaves the corner store
headed
towards
pain,
which will be
inflicted
by the gang
just because he
incorrectly
shook the hand
of the little man
strapped
with
Anger,
who was waiting
on the opportunity
to seek unity
with his banger,
for His Savior
said
find
your
Joy.

And when they
direct disrespect,
then with toys
made for men
you will bless
them
and not little boys
because the
Pain
for their mother
might be too hard
to bare,
being that might
be the only one
she has here.

At this point
Anger
should not override
reason...
so, don't let it
start this season
because
some are already
bleeding
on the inside
with
Joy,
aroused from
the clouds
dispersing
a brand new
baby girl and boy.

YOU'RE NOT CRAZY
by Lance Thompson

I always thought depression was just a feeling of sadness. But I never knew what depression was until I experienced it myself. In 2008, I had my first bout with depression and the feeling I felt was much deeper than (just) sadness.

Depression felt like a paralyzing energy I could only escape from temporarily by sleeping. I slept a lot. I wasn't motivated to do anything. I didn't like being around people because of this never-ending feeling. In fact, I would call in sick from work and tried isolating myself from everyone. At the time, I didn't know I was depressed – all the time. I just knew I wasn't feeling like myself.

I moved to Georgia with Olivia, my former wife. Our move to another state gave me something to get excited about. I silently hoped our decision to move would change the way I felt inside. For a little while, moving to the "Bible Belt" gave me some relief. But the ominous feeling of depression came right back. My depression was so bad I was compelled to (finally) take my wife's advice, seek help and visit a therapist.

Initially, I didn't want to go to therapy because I didn't want people to think I was "crazy." Historically, in the Black community people often believe therapy is where "crazy" people are sent. Nonetheless, going to see a therapist regularly helped me a lot. In fact, after I was diagnosed with depression I decided to learn more about mental illness and studied diligently about it. The more I learned the less I felt I was "crazy."

I learned depression was present in my family. I learned my great grandfather suffered from depression – and died by suicide. I learned my grandfather might have died the same way. I learned how depression painfully impacted my family, and I became motivated to get better, for myself and my children.

After becoming educated about depression, its symptoms and possible solutions, I was inspired to share my knowledge with others - particularly Black men who experience the same challenges. I was blessed to appear on CNN and talk about my personal journey living with depression. My intention there was to (hopefully) save a life.

Depression is a mental illness and should be treated as such. I still have bouts of depression but today I know how to manage it: after being in therapy. Part of my self-care regiment includes cutting back on sugar, drinking plenty of water, eating live foods, getting sunlight and staying physically active.

I think it's very important to find a person, or people, you feel safe with and trust to share your innermost thoughts and feelings. I've also learned it's very important to "get out of your head" and talk with empathetic and understanding people. Cultivating support is one of the keys to battling depression.

VULNERABILITY IS STRENGTH
by Jevon Wooden

I suffer from depression and Post-Traumatic Stress Disorder (PTSD). I looked for peace in places where only trouble could be found, such as the bottom of a liquor bottle, or in a woman whose trauma (also) needed to be addressed. I blacked out from alcohol to not remember feeling the emotional pain and sleepless nightmares again. I tried ignoring my mental health struggles by living as if everything was okay. I learned those behaviors did more harm than good. Eventually I sought professional help and learned to become vulnerable.

Vulnerability is the true key to healing.

When you are vulnerable, you are open to help from others. It becomes freeing to share your story with others, especially your loved ones. You learn not to keep yourself in the internal prison your soul feels confined in while you're in this constant battle with your mental health issues. Healing cannot take place without getting the help you need.

I believe we need to normalize saying "I'm not okay."

Ideally there should be no judgment for being human. Our struggles are not unique, but what could be unique would be for us to share our struggles. A study by the American Foundation for Suicide Prevention found in 2020 men died by suicide 3.6 times more than women. When you consider both genders, 90% of their suicides had a diagnosable mental health condition before their demise. In the Black community, suicide rates have steadily risen in the last decade.

What do I glean from these disturbing statistics? In my opinion, many of these deaths are preventable. We can begin to change the narrative within our community - starting with ourselves. Black men aren't used to being vulnerable; most of us are taught its "weak" to cry or show real emotion. Black men are taught to hold everything in and "suck it up." What good has that done? What benefits do we see from holding in pain until it boils over into anger? What fruits have we produced from damaged relationships: byproducts of our lack of self-love and emotional intelligence?

The answer: none.

I'm here to tell you real strength lies in being authentically you and sharing your truth. I believe when you share your truth, you will find your purpose in life. I believe you will also find solace in others who only desire healing and happiness for your soul. But none of this can happen before your personal commitment to emotional vulnerability.

When I was younger, I was afraid to ask for help, thinking I couldn't show "weakness" and I had to get everything done on my own. I didn't want to be a burden to my family or friends or be seen as "weak." Yet, I was conflicted with the idea those who loved me wouldn't help me or couldn't help me – which led me down a dark path.

I had anger issues because I didn't know why living was so hard. I had no clue my mental health was under siege by depression. Growing up, my life seemed to be consumed with heartache. In fact, during my senior year of high school my anger and frustration with being poor and feeling misunderstood reached a boiling point. I was arrested at age 17, facing seven years in prison. Thankfully, by the grace of God, I avoided serious time: my pain was my turning point. I realized I couldn't be successful without professional help.

I've endured other struggles in my life, including my dependency on alcohol as a coping mechanism. The only way I overcame the adversity was by getting professional help. Black men have to stop being reactive and start becoming proactive when it comes to addressing our mental health. I see a therapist regularly.

Today, I am the founder of Live Not Loathe, LLC, a mindset and perception coaching firm with a focus on Black men whose trauma holds them back from a life of fulfillment and purpose. I consciously decided to define my own legacy.

I believe true freedom can only be achieved when you are in the right frame of mind – one of abundance. I challenge Black men to do the (internal) work necessary to unlock your power. I also implore Black men to open up your hearts and minds and let your story be known. In helping yourself, you will also help others to realize, sometimes, it is okay to not be okay.

Vulnerability is the true key to healing.

BLACK MEN AND MENTAL HEALTH: A SPIRITUAL PERSPECTIVE

by Dr. Demoine Kinney

I am a Black Man.
I am a son.
I am a brother.
I am a friend.
I am a husband.
I am a parent.
I am a War Veteran.
I am a Pastor.

I have several decades of varied life experiences and feel blessed to share my journey. My father transitioned when I was six years old. I know how it feels to grow up with a void which can make you feel unworthy of life's abundant blessings. A void can sometimes lead to self-destructive behavior.

I know how it feels to come home from a military experience in a war and it seems like no one wants you around. I also suffered from Post-Traumatic Stress Disorder (PTSD) and didn't want to be around other people. I wanted to isolate myself from the world but knew it was necessary to be in the company of someone – and not suffer in silence.

I know how it feels to believe you have destroyed your life so completely to the point of no return. I fathered a child outside the sacredness of marriage. I had to "man up" in court and prove I'm a trustworthy parent to my son.

I have endured numerous personal challenges in my life. I'm still here. Many of us weather difficult times in life but have no idea how to navigate it all. My faith helped me get through everything. I came to know my Creator utilizing a simple daily practice.

When I was deployed in Kuwait I learned, among other lessons, not to try and force things into existence but allow the Creator to orchestrate every move and just follow His lead. Many people think you will find this practice in church but that wasn't true for me.

I discovered the truth about God during my service efforts in Kuwait. He spoke to my spirit and said, *"You are fighting what I have purposed for your life."* But when I attended church and candidly revealed some of my circumstances and issues, people told me, *"Don't claim that! That is not of God!"*

In church I was never told what to do. God inspired me to stop relying solely on prayer and incorporate meditation: His time to speak directly to my heart and soul. 12 years ago I began meditating regularly. I studied the practice of meditation and the life visioning process. Never confuse church and/or religion with spirituality; these concepts are by no means similar.

The church wants to reject God's will. Spirituality embraces His will fully. We must embrace our true authentic self – which can only happen through spiritual experiences with Our Creator. After I began my daily meditation practices, I realized there were (and are) many people who had never been in a war. Yet they shared the same conditions and those conditions are not to make us weaker but stronger.

I learned every situation in life doesn't happen to us: it happens for us. I learned our story isn't for us but for the next generation coming behind us. We can teach them how we made it through. Finally, I learned to affirm myself daily. I want to encourage you to do the same and start each day with the following affirmations:

I am enough.
I am here on purpose.
I will live on purpose.
I am courageous.
I am strong.
I am beautiful.
I am talented.
I am a King.
I have dominion over the Earth.
I am above and not beneath.
I can have all the Creator purposed me to have.
I am worthy of a great life full of peace and love.

I suggest you affirm yourself every day and watch how your life changes. You are worthy!

THE YEAR OF NO
by Michael Ward

December 31, 2020, I was alone in a Miami hotel room sleeping through rounds of fireworks to usher in a new year. I was exhausted. I wanted a full night sleep badly. My therapist and I outlined a self-care plan. I had to leave Atlanta, specifically my bedroom, to get overdue rest. She suggested I spend time by the water. I often told her water slows me down. *"You need a break even if you just drive and sit in the car at the beach,"* she said. I also need to establish life and work boundaries. Ironically, of all places, I chose South Beach - to rest.

I was an emotional wreck. I felt blessed to be living my dreams, but didn't have time to be present in most of the moments. I felt guilty I was everywhere yet not showing up in my relationships. I felt like I was failing my friends. I wasn't able to sleep more than a few hours without my mind racing. Could I make every interview, every audition, every acting gig, friend's night out, birthday celebrations, date nights, etc.? Would they be mad if I didn't show? Do they think I think I'm better than them because I'm not there?

I felt dried up. I felt like a fraud; smiling week after week on camera except behind my smile I was trying to hold myself together just like everyone else during moments of uncertainty. My calendar ran my life. I need to slow down and process my feelings. I could no longer hear my own voice. Most importantly, I need to follow my own advice.

I need to set boundaries and learn to say no.

Ever since childhood I found comfort in my bedroom. During the pandemic, my sanctuary became a base camp for everything. Working the corporate nine-to-five at home gave me flexibility. Yet, I was expected to perform at a higher level of productivity. COVID-19 slowed the world down, but I was moving faster than ever. I acted virtually, took over hosting duties, and started a Black affinity space to center Black queer film, television and theatre.

I performed in some of the most challenging but rewarding productions of my acting career. I love playing Black queer characters – we need more representation of the totality of our humanity. Yes, there's pain and trauma, which is a part of life, but let's make room for joy and love. I'm thankful to work with incredible Black men who excel in their gifts.

Thandiwe DeShazor directed a virtual reading of Donja R. Love's One in Two for Out Front Theatre. The play tells the stories of Black men living with HIV. Upon reading the script for the first time, I cried. I knew these characters. This is my life. I was afraid of taking on such a huge task, but I channeled my fear to energize these performances. I'll never forget that experience.

Monte J. Wolfe of Brave Soul Collective organized Black Men Feel, an incredible three-part series to capture the mental health experiences of Black men through artistic work. I partnered closely with Monte on a monologue about a Black gay man's first therapy session. We talked for hours about our therapy experiences and life. He reassured me during this project: my life experience wasn't isolated. I'm grateful for moments when I feel heard, seen, and acknowledged by other Black gay men. In my 30s, I realize how important this is to my overall mental health and well-being.

The universe brought me and Josh Jenks together. We formed BLACK, GAY, stuck at home (BGSAH), a Black queer affinity space. Josh and I host a bi-weekly virtual screening night of upcoming Black queer creators while uplifting pioneers of Black LGBT films with the cast and crew of their work present to drop gems while everyone chats.

We evolved the space to end with a virtual dance party to celebrate our lives. BGSAH offers people connection during a time where many Black gay bars and spaces are closing. Working alongside Josh to bring a few hours of joy to a marginalized community reaffirmed my belief Black queer friendships exist.

I took over hosting duties for Revolutionary Health, a virtual show to highlight Black gay men's health and wellness. Every week I invite the audience into my bedroom where guests and I chat about issues affecting the Black gay community. In December 2020 I was interviewed by Dr. David Malebranche for Revolutionary Health about my journey with mental health. During the conversation, I talked openly about my childhood experiences with a church therapist after a traumatic family event.

My teenage rebellious self couldn't engage with the process. Reflecting now on my pain then, I didn't realize my parents did the best they could from their life perspectives. Essentially, they wanted to make sure I was alright. But I figured this experience was an extension of their religious beliefs: homosexuality is a sin God needs to remove. After retelling the story, I felt I betrayed their childhood rule, "what goes on in this house stays in this house." It was tough but I did it anyway. Still, I think rules which cause people to suffer in silence deserve to be broken.

> *"When you believe in things*
> *That you don't understand,*
> *Then you suffer,*
> *Superstition ain't the way."*
> *— Stevie Wonder, Superstition, Jobete Music, October 1972.*

When I knew the interviews would go public I sent a group text message to my family. I wanted them to know I considered their individual feelings. Over the next few days, I had conversations with my family about our various mental health journeys. Sharing my story inspired many important conversations with my parents and sisters. I wanted decades of family pain resolved in a single phone call, but it wasn't. I'm committed to my work in therapy with those issues.

2020 taught me valuable lessons. I learned more visibility sparks more criticism and praise. I'm thankful our show is positively received. Also, there are some negative comments posted about me (and in response to some of the show's topics). I asked my therapist, *"What do I do with all of these feelings because I have to continue doing this work? I want to make sure I'm going to be able to last through this."*

My therapist and I developed healthy coping strategies. Journaling helps me address complex feelings in an uncensored way. Between the journal pages I'm learning to free myself from self-judgment. Also, my relationship with social media has changed. I give myself permission to live in the moment, and, when necessary, disconnect from social media - to be fully present.

Today, I have an urgency to live more authentic than ever. There are many dreams I want to explore before I transition. I love my work, but to avoid burnout I must check in with myself first, and foremost. Now, I ask myself: how will this decision benefit me and the world around me?

After saying yes to almost every opportunity which presented itself last year, I'm growing more confident in saying no without fear of losing a colleague or a once in a lifetime opportunity. My support system and tribe remind me to set aside quality time to pour into myself. I prioritize happiness, joy, and love as best I can. In those moments when I feel overwhelmed I can gently remind myself I'm still a work in progress.

Alvin Smith

My name is Alvin Smith. I was born and raised in the village of Harlem. My creative talents include acting, essays, martial arts, and poetry. I was a featured performer at different venues in New York City, including the *Apollo Theater, Brooklyn Moon Café, Imagenation Cinema, Joe's Public Theater,* and *Nuyorican Poets Café.*

As a playwright, I starred in and wrote *Raw Materials*, a one-man play, directed by John Bentham and Gregory Gates. Also, I was a production assistant with Ground Zero. I humbly received my G.E.D. in January 2020.

Ayoinomotion

Ayoinmotion, is a uniquely dynamic performance artist whose delivery and stage mastery set ablaze the legendary Essence Festival 25th Anniversary Edition which featured global hip hop icons, Mary J. Blige, Nas, Missy Elliot, and Former First Lady Michelle Obama. He collaborated with Apple for their esteemed *Today at Apple* series, where he curated and screened his stunning Ifemelu-Americanah visual for a sold-out audience. His latest EP, SOVA, within three months of its release surpassed 72,000 streams.

Ayo is also a passionate poet who believes in using his artistic platform as a vehicle for social action. He organized a benefit for the kidnapped Nigerian girls. He performed with his band to raise funds for children affected by contaminated lead water in Flint, Michigan. His essay as a Nigerian immigrant coming of age in Flint juxtaposed with the water crisis was exclusively featured in Huffington Post.

Brandon Bolden

Brandon Bolden, Licensed Marriage and Family Therapist in Colorado and Texas, specializes in trauma, life transitions, interpersonal/intrapersonal relationships, and life coaching. He earned his Master Degree in Marriage and Family Therapy at Abilene Christian University and is now completing his Ph.D. at the University of Louisiana at Monroe. Brandon prides himself in his ability to methodically create spaces of healing and growth by drawing from a wealth of experiences. His secret: "When in doubt, go slow."

Outside of the therapy arena, Brandon enjoys vegan cooking, video gaming, random excursions, and entertaining through song and dance (his wife and two fur babies reap the benefits). His quick wit allows him to learn prudently and seamlessly connect with other people. Brandon credits the crux of his character to family, friends, and mentors who made incredible sacrifices for him in his life and taught him valuable life lessons.

Charles Crouch

Charles Crouch, 44, was born in Winston-Salem, North Carolina. Charles is an author, filmmaker, mental health advocate, musician, and poet. He was a Psychology Major at North Carolina Central University. Charles has authored five books. Also, he produced a documentary titled, *"I'm Good Bro: Unmasking Black Male Depression,"* with his company 4C Visuals Group and his business partner Corbin Coleman.

Charles resides in Raleigh, North Carolina with his son Charles Jordan.

Craig Washington

Craig Washington was born and raised by Anna and Leon Washington in Queens, New York and has lived in Atlanta, Georgia since 1992. Craig is a prolific writer and licensed social worker. He has written extensively on matters essential to Black LGBTQ and HIV+ people for numerous publication such as *TheBody.com, Huffington Post, The Atlanta Voice, Georgia Voice, POZ.com, Atlanta Magazine,* and *The Advocate.*

Craig has also written for various anthologies including *Black Gay Genius: Answering Joseph Beam's Call,* and the upcoming project, *Cultural Silence and Wounded Souls: Black Men Speak About Mental Health.* Craig has created and/or participated in several HIV prevention and cultural education programs. He is a long-term survivor: diagnosed HIV+ over 30 years.

He can be reached at twitter.com/craigwerks
and craigwerks13060@gmail.com

David Malebranche

David Malebranche, MD, MPH, is a board-certified internal medicine physician with expertise in sexual health and HIV/STI prevention and treatment. David is a public health official, activist, and educator who lives in Atlanta, Georgia. He appears in the YouTube series *"Revolutionary Health"* as part of The Counter Narrative Project and on the #AskTheHIVDoc video series.

Dr. Malebranche's writings and research have been published in JAMA, the Annals of Internal Medicine, the American Journal of Public Health, and Lancet. In 2015 he penned a memoir titled, "Standing on His Shoulders," about his relationship with his father, available on Amazon.

Devan Dmarcus

Devan Dmarcus Dunson is a multi-faceted artist, entrepreneur and community activist. Devan is best known for his work as former Co-Director of the international organization *Black Men Smile* and Founder of *The Heart Werk, Inc.* He dedicates his life's work to helping others find and cultivate their unique talents.

As an educator, Devan has led keynote discussions and workshops at many higher learning institutions such as Emory University, University of Georgia, University of Arizona, and Western Illinois University. His work was featured in, and on Essence Magazine, CNN, BET, USA, VH1, and OWN. Devan encourages global citizens to commit to the pursuit of their true passions and he also strives to leave a positive impact on the world transcending others' lifetimes.

For more info about Devan please visit www.theheartwerk.com

Donnie Hill

Donnie Hill intimately knows the heartache, shame, and trauma which results from internalizing and suppressing pain. At 20 years old, Donnie contemplated suicide after struggling for years with depression. After checking himself into a hospital for one week, he knew he could no longer endure suffering in silence. A few days later, he decided he wanted a new way to live.

Today, Donnie is the CEO and Founder of *Life Maximizer, LLC*, a business and marketing strategy consulting company. Donnie combines life lessons he learned through his education at Stanford University, along with his experience as a business growth strategist and facilitator, communication coach, and leadership development specialist to help leaders and their communities build long-term and meaningful change. Despite the chaos and disruption in the world, his mission is to serve others, foster daily joy, create positive impacts and ignite souls!

Dr. Demoine Kinney

Dr. Demoine Kinney is the quintessential Renaissance man: author, comedian, developer, entrepreneur, founder, media personality, and transformational speaker. His global platform has reached and served nearly 30 million people.

Dr. Kinney was a disabled war veteran (Kuwait) struggling with PTSD – and became a humble millionaire. He's appeared on Club 36, Live with Kelly, Nite-Line, and The Atlanta Live. Dr. Kinney is also a Reverend. He lives, plays, and works in Atlanta, Georgia.

Dr. Kinney founded a nonprofit foundation, *Warriors Operation Healing, Inc.* They successfully impacted the lives of 25,000 service members and veterans; prevented over 2,000 teen suicides; supported 2,500 college students and helped thousands of folks reunite their families.

Dr. Obari Cartman

Dr. Obari Cartman is a father, son, brother, uncle, thinker, writer, therapist, photographer, drummer, and grassroots mental health advocate. A Chicago native, his cultural and educational foundations were cultivated by several African-centered institutions. He received his undergraduate degree from Hampton University and a Ph.D. in Clinical and Community Psychology from Georgia State University. His recent work includes being a trauma focused clinician and restorative justice coach with H.E.L.P. LLC (Healing Empowering and Learning Professions) in Chicago public schools.

Dr. Cartman served as a Professor of Psychology at Georgia State University and the Carruthers Center for Inner City Studies at Northeastern University. He recently created a male rites of passage curriculum, MANifest, which is being implemented in juvenile detention centers, schools, and in private community settings. Currently, he is Program Director for Real Men Charities, Inc., where he facilitates weekly men's wellness and African drumming circles.

Dr. Cartman is the immediate past President of the Chicago Association of Black Psychologists, where he developed a directory of Black mental health providers. As a valued consultant, he facilitates trainings for adults and workshops with youth centered on maintaining good mental health, critical analysis of hip hop and media, racial and cultural diversity, developing authentic manhood, and healthy relationships.

Dr. T. Hasan Johnson

Dr. T. Hasan Johnson is an Associate Professor of Africana Studies at California State University, Fresno. Dr. Johnson earned his doctorate at Claremont Graduate University, his M.A. at Temple University, and his B.A. at California State University, Dominguez Hills.

Dr. Johnson founded numerous Fresno State programs including *The Africana Studies Online Teleconference on Black Male Studies, The ONYX Black Male Film Festival, The Black popular Culture Lecture Series and Online Research Archive* (curator), *The ONYX Black Male Collective, The Annual ASHE': Sankofa Black Film Festival, The Annual Africana Studies Black Gender Conference, The African American Edge Initiative (co-founder), The Africana Studies Black Elder Project,* and *The Hip-Hop Research & Interview Project.*

Dr. Johnson is the developer of the concept of *"Black Masculinism"* and frequently publishes on anti-Black misandry, anti-Black male heterophobia, intra-racial misandry, and White supremacy. His first book, *You Must Learn!: A Primer for the Study of Hip-Hop* (2012), examines the socio-political histories which contribute to the development of Hip-Hop culture and creates new theoretical frameworks for understanding its development.

Jason Rosario

Jason Rosario serves as Chief Diversity, Equity & Inclusion Officer at BBDO where he leads the agency's vision of building an intersectional and inclusive creative agency. An Afro-Latino native New Yorker, Jason's multicultural perspective informs his quintessential ability for radical empathy and vulnerability.

In 2017 Jason founded The Lives of Men (TLoM), a social impact agency which explores themes around masculinity, psychological safety, and identity. He also serves on the board of Made of Millions, a nonprofit organization changing negative stigmas around mental health. He also Executive Produced and hosted the Yahoo! News original web series "Dear Men," featuring conversations with producer/rapper Swizz Beatz, NBA champion Kevin Love, and other influencers focused on their views of masculinity in a post #MeToo world.

Jeff Rocker

Born and raised in Miami, Florida, Jeff J. Rocker is the founder and CEO of *How We See It, Inc.* Jeff established a team of diverse individuals who are "changing the world's perspective on mental health one community at a time." He created an outreach program called *Hip Hop Therapy*, an interactive workshop done in high schools across South Florida. His goal is for students to utilize a safe space to express themselves in an unconventional manner.

Prior to the birth of HWSI, Mr. Rocker organized lectures and various events in the community, including excursions and retreats for couples to improve their communication and gain mutual understanding. Jeff has also worked with clients in the sports and music industry to improve their performance in high level moments.

Mr. Rocker is a Licensed Mental Health Counselor. Jeff earned his Master's Degree from Nova Southeaster and his Bachelor's Degree from Bethune Cookman University. He's in the process of earning his Ph.D. in Marriage and Family Therapy from Nova Southeastern University.

Jevon Wooden

Jevon Wooden was born and raised in Rochester, New York. Jevon overcame adversity, becoming a successful entrepreneur and cybersecurity professional. But he was arrested and faced seven years in prison at 17. While incarcerated he realized he needed to change – and God answered his prayers. He served in the U.S. Army reserve for 12 years, deploying overseas three times. He was awarded a Bronze Star Medal for heroic acts during a suicide bombing.

Jevon earned a Bachelor's Degree in Information Technology from the American Public University System, a Master's Degree in Cybersecurity from Fordham University, and an MBA from the University of Maryland, Robert H. Smooth School of Business. He's a warrior against mental health issues; he lives with depression and PTSD. He's an advocate for the Black community fighting for racial equity. He's also founder of Live Not Loathe, LLC, a mindset and perception coaching firm devoted to helping Black men obtain the "purposeful, fulfilling life they deserve."

Jevon enjoys spending quality time in nature, learning, traveling, live music, and performing community service.

Jonathan Mathias Lassiter, Ph.D.

Jonathan Mathias Lassiter, Ph.D. is a polymath who utilizes psychology, writing, and dance to help others heal and thrive. His roles include licensed clinical psychologist, professor, author, public speaker, and choreographer. As a public intellectual, Dr. Lassiter has been featured on television, radio, podcasts, and print media such as PBS and Sirius XM.

Dr. Lassiter is the award-winning co-editor of Black LGBT Health in the United States: The Intersection of Race, Gender, and Sexual Orientation. This book received the Gay and Lesbian Medical Association's Achievement Award. It is the first and only text focused solely on Black LGBT American's holistic health. Jonathan is working on his first sole-authored book which explores contemporary issues of race and mental health in the United States.

Currently, Dr. Lassiter is Assistant Professor of Psychology at Rowan University, Visiting Assistant Professor of Medicine at University of California, San Francisco, and Artistic Associate at The Black Acting Methods Studio.

Josh Odam

Josh Odam is the founder and curator of *Healing While Black*, an online platform devoted to normalizing conversations around mental health for Black and Indigenous queer, trans*, and gender non-conforming people. Currently, Josh is pursuing a Master of Social Work (MSW) and has launched his trauma-informed life coaching practice. Josh understands his mental health is inextricably linked to antiblackness and queer antagonism. His goal is to provide comprehensive and holistic therapeutic intervention for marginalized communities. His work has been featured in Essence, The Nation, America Hates Us, Buzzfeed, and New Sincerity.

Keith Mascoll

Keith Mascoll SAG-AFTRA, AEA, is an actor, producer, mental health advocate, sneaker head, and Founder of the Triggered Project. He is Co-Host of the *Living a Triggered Life* Podcast with his wife Roxanne, and a Luminary for the Isabella Stewart Gardner Museum. Keith has a New York Critics Choice Award for his work on stage. Keith strives to use his art for social change in the Black and Brown community. As a survivor of sexual abuse, he intends to help end the stigma which surrounds mental health; and Black and Brown men talking about being abused.

Keith is committed to using his unique and innovative style of storytelling to engender love, laughter, and empathy in each story told. Also, Keith is Co-Founder of a professional black theater company, *The Front Porch Arts Collective,* and a teaching Artist with the August Wilson Monologue Competition. Look for Keith in the lead role in the movie, *Confused by Love,* on Amazon Prime, and as Applesauce in The polka King, on Netflix.

To learn more about Keith, visit www.keithmascoll.com.

Lance Thompson

Comedian Lance Thompson is originally from Lexington Park, Maryland. Thompson began his creative journey in Washington, DC in 2006. Lance has performed all over the nation and shared the stage with *Joe Clair from WPGC 95.5, Griff from Praise 104.1, Rodney Perry,* and many other talented comedians.

Lance was once featured on the radio show *Get Up!* Mornings with Erica Campbell, the multi-award winning gospel artist from the sister duo Mary Mary. As an event host, Lance is well known for his gifted poetry, which he showcased while hosting various open mics in Baltimore, Maryland and Washington, DC.

Michael Ward

Michael Ward is an Atlanta-based actor, writer, and advocate. Michael has numerous movies, online, and stage appearances to his credit. He is the host of *Revolutionary Health,* a program by the Counter Narrative Project, which focuses on Black gay men's health and overall wellness. Michael is co-founder of the BLACK, GAY, stuck at home series, an online screening and interview series created to uplift Black, queer film, television, and theatre artists.

Monte J. Wolfe

Monte J. Wolfe is an actor, writer, director, producer, musician, and activist. Monte is also an experienced theatre professional with an extensive background in theatre management, arts administration, and production. He has worked professionally in the Washington, DC metropolitan area since 1999. He is a trained actor and singer with various stage, film, and television appearances to his credit. Monte is a graduate of the Howard University Theatre Arts Department, where he earned a BFA in Theatre Arts Administration in 1999.

Monte is the Founder, Artistic and Managing Director of *Brave Soul Collective* (BSC), an arts, education, and outreach organization with a focus on HIV/AIDS and issues affecting the lives of LGBTQ people, through the performing and healing arts. Through his BSC work, Monte has served as a producer, director, and playwright for numerous theatrical productions, and community events since 2006.

For more info on Monte and Brave Soul Collective,
visit www.WeAreBraveSouls.com

Mychal Sledge

Mychal Sledge is the Co-founder and CEO of *The Sledge Group, Inc.,* a unique nonprofit community-based, family-oriented program which provides male and female adolescent mentoring groups, tutorial services and a support network for the parents of the youth who participate. The Sledge Group, Inc. strives to empower, uplift and foster meaningful changes in the lives of urban youth. For more info: sledgegroup@aol.com

Mychal is a servant of God, husband, father, published writer and world renowned martial artist. Mychal traveled globally as an elite member of the United States Karate Team, winning several National and International championships, including two goal medals in the Pan-American Games. He attained unprecedented status upon being listed in the World Almanac five consecutive years.

Mychal is available for speaking engagements and workshops covering a myriad of topics.

Myles J. Robinson

Myles J. Robinson is a Director at *Chick-fil-A The Grove*, a $7.4 million volume restaurant in Hoover, Alabama. Myles held a myriad of positions in the sport industry before pivoting to his current role in hospitality.

Myles attended the University of North Carolina at Chapel Hill on a full merit-based academic scholarship. At UNC, he was recognized at the Michigan Sport Business Conference as one of the top 10 undergraduates in sport business.

A dynamic communicator, Myles, 27, is known for his innate ability to collaborate with intentionality and connect with hearts and minds. He recently took a role as the Social Media Manager for the *Center for Sport Business and Analytics,* a Chapel Hill-based sport industry startup company. He lives in Birmingham, Alabama and is training for his third half marathon.

Percival Fisher

Percival Fisher, Jr. is a Licensed Clinical Social Worker (LCSW) in California, Pennsylvania and Washington. In addition to his licensure, Percival is a Board-Certified Diplomate in Clinical Social Work (BCD) of the American Board of Examiners in Clinical Social Work. Also, he is a Certified Complex Trauma Professional (CCTP-II) from the International Association of Trauma Professionals and a Certified Case Manager (CCM) from the Commission for Case Management Certification.

Regarding his extensive clinical work, Percival has experience providing individual psychotherapy and group psychotherapy for over 10 years. Additionally, he offers a plethora of experience in various settings, which include acute care, behavioral health research, HIV/AIDS education, and counseling, leadership, medical social work, and teaching.

Reginald Howard

Reginald A. Howard is a Mental Health Activist. Reg uses his life experiences to ignite, inspire and empower others to prioritize their mental health. He was featured on *Comcast, CNBC, The Philadelphia Tribune*, and *Voyage Magazine*. On a typical day, his contributions include being an active board member for Lindley Academy Charter School, presentations for the *National Alliance on Mental Illness* and serving as Senior Program Coordinator for *Black Men Heal*.

Reg went through the first cohort of Black Men Heal and is a real-life example of a healed man healing other men. Whether through his emotionally connecting speeches, mentally healing podcast, or paradigm shifting book, Reg puts the motivation into mental health to make it the focal point of today's conversation. His personal story furthers his mission to not only impact his community but people everywhere. From middle schools to police departments, he intends to be of service and leave the world better than he found it.

Richard Rowe

Richard A. Rowe is a project consultant for *The Black Mental Health Alliance for Education and Consultation, Inc. (BMHA)*, and is responsible for providing strategic guidance and assistance to staff in the planning and implementing of special activities/educational forums, community engagement interventions and training sessions to inform and promote BMHA's vision, mission and goals with youth, parents, Black men and other community members and organizations.

Richard enjoys reading, listening to jazz music, visiting African American museums, and writing essays, Op-Ed articles, and poetry. He also enjoys spending quality time with his family and taking time out – whenever possible – to meditate and enjoy quiet moments. Richard is the author of *"Wanted Black Fathers: Only Serious Black Men Need Apply."*

Please email Richard at rrowe84@aol.com, or go to:
https://blackmentalhealth.com.

Ronald Dodzro

Ronald Dodzro is a Black and British man with ancestral origins from Ghana and Togo. Ronald is a Trainee Clinical Psychologist. His aim in the profession is to shake up the status quo. He believes our society needs more clinical psychologists who represent all the communities they serve, not just the Eurocentric ones.

Ronald serves the African and Caribbean communities, who are less likely to receive treatment for anxiety disorders and depression, but are more likely to be diagnosed with schizophrenia, or are detained under the Mental Health Act. Ronald serves the men who are less likely – because of toxic masculinity – to access mental health services than women, but are more likely to die by suicide. This is his duty and his narrative!

Steven G. Fullwood

Steven G. Fullwood is a writer, archivist, photographer, and filmmaker. His published works include Black Gay Genius: Answering Joseph Beam's Call (co-edited with Charles Stephens, 2014), and Carry the Word: A Bibliography of Black LGBTQ Books (co-edited with Lisa C. Moore, 2007).

Public Archivist][Independent Contractor][Filmmaker

The Nomadic Archivists Project (NAP)

NAP Twitter

Email: steven@nomadicarchivistsproject.com

Twitter: @stevengfullwood

Facebook: Steven G Fullwood

Terrance Coffie

Terrance Coffie is a 2017 Master of Social Work (MSW) and 2016 Bachelor of Social Work (BSW) graduate of New York University (NYU). In 2017 Terrance was named the *Alex Rosen NASW NYC-NYU Student of the Year,* and the *2017 Citizens Against Recidivism, Educator of the Year.* Also, he was NYU's *2016 President Service Award Recipient.*

As a social justice advocate, youth activist, and proponent for educational and criminal justice reform, Terrance is committed to being a change agent via higher education. Terrance currently teaches Forensic Justice in Problem Solving Courts at New York University. He is the founder of *Educate Don't Incarcerate; Director of the I Am A Credible Messenger National Campaign,* contributing author in *Race, Education* and *Reintegrating the Formerly Incarcerated Citizen.* Terrance is one of the foremost leading voices on criminal justice reform in the United States.

Tim'm West

Tim'm West is a native of Cincinnati, Ohio, raised in Little Rock, and Taylor, Arkansas. Tim'm is an educator, hip hop artist, poet and youth advocate who has traveled for decades across the U.S. to speak about issues of gender, race, sexuality, and social justice. A proud graduate of Duke University (B.A.), The New School for Social Research (M.A.), and Stanford University (M.A.), he authored several books, hip hop projects and is widely anthologized.

In 2004 Tim'm started the *Front Porch:* a performance art series mobilizing hundreds of artists for over a decade. He appeared in multiple documentaries centered around Black masculinity and hip hop – *Pick Up The Mic* by Alex Hinton, *Hip Hop: Beyond Beats and Rhymes,* by Byron Hurt, and *Bring Your 'A' Game,* by Mario Van Peebles. In 2015 he released his fourth book, *pre | dispositions: a poetic memoir,* with a chapter on his experiences as an educator.

Tim'm served as inaugural faculty at Oakland School for the Arts. He impacted educational outcomes as a basketball coach and English teacher at Cesar Chavez Public Charter High School for Public Policy, and recently, as Director of Youth Services at Center on Halsted. In October 2016 Tim'm released his sixth solo hip hop/soul project, ICONography. During that same month, he was named 2015 *LGBT History Month Icon.*

Currently, Tim'm leads *Teach for America's national LGBTQ Community Initiative*, advancing braver and safer classrooms for LGBTQ students, PreK-12, and their educators. In 2017 he decided to better capture his holistic experiences as a celebrated Renaissance Man. Tim'm migrated the virtual home for his life's work to www.braveeducator.com: a broader portal mobilizing his innovation and leadership in creative, educational and social justice spheres.

Ulrick Accime

Ulrick "Jay" Accime is a licensed clinical social worker (CSW 14411). Jay is the founder of *KAI Wellness Center*. He began practicing in the mental health field in 2014. His experience includes serving adolescents and adults with severe mental illness. Jay earned his BSW from Florida Atlantic University and later earned his MSW from Barry University. As founder of KAI Wellness Center, his work is centered on adult males with anxiety and depression. Jay is also a Qualified Supervisor for social work interns.

For more info, please visit: www.kaiwellnesscenter.com

RESOURCES

Books

12 Books on Mental and Emotional Health by Blackety Black Folks	by Alexander Hardy
A Better Him	by BJ Thompson
All Boys Aren't Blue	by George M. Johnson
Black Men and Depression	by John Head
Black Mental Health Matters: The Ultimate Guide For Mental Health Awareness in the Black Community	by Aaren Snyder
Black Pain: It Just Looks Like We're Not Hurting	by Terrie Williams
Dear Black Son, A Written For One Series	by Keena S. White
Good Mornings	by Dr. Randolph Sconiers
Heavy: An American Memoir	by Kiese Laymon
I Found Me	by Corey Hall
Injured Reserve: A Black Man's Playbook to Manage Being Sidelined by Mental Illness	by Rwenshaun Miller
Invisible Man: Got the Whole World Watching	by Mychal Denzel Smith
I Too Am America On Loving and Leading Black Men & Boys	by Shawn Dove and Nick Chiles
Man, Just Express Yourself	by James Harris
Mental Health Among African Americans: Innovations In Research and Practice	by Dr. Erlanger A. Turner
My Grandmother's Hands: Racialized Trauma and The Pathway to Mending Our Hearts and Minds	by Resmaa Menakem
Own Your Kingdom How to Control Your Mindset So You Can Control Your Destiny	by Jevon Wooden
Suffering Into Success	by Reginald A. Howard
The Other Side: Freedom from Depression & Suicide	by Richard Taylor, Jr.
The Passage	by B. Musique Cooks
The Unapologetic Guide to Black Mental Health	by Rheeda Walker, Ph.D.
Untold: Testimony and Guide to Overcoming Adversity	by Leon Ford

Hashtags

#amplifyblackvoice
#blackclinicians
#blackhealing
#blackmentalhealth
#blackmentalhealthprofessional
#blackobsidian
#blackpsychology
#blackselfcare
#blacktherapist
#cliniciansofcolor
#docndadudeanswers
#healingjourney
#melanatedsocialwork
#racialtrauma
#suicideprevention
#theheartwerk
#whatsgoodbro
#yougoodman?

#blackboyjoy
#blackdoctors
#blackkingsneedtherapytoo
#blackmentalhealthmatters
#blackmentalwellness
#blackprotest
#blackresistance
#blacksolidarity
#blacktherapy
#culturalcompetence
#essencewellnesshouse
#keeptheconversationgoing
#pocmentalhealthmatters
#racism
#thecounselingbrothersofatlanta
#theonlywayoutisthrough
#whyeustressin

Helplines & Hotlines

Crisis Text Line:	Text "home" to 741741
Disaster Distress Helpline	1-800-985-5990
Domestic Violence Hotline	1-888-565-8860
LGBT National Hotline	*www.lgbthotline.org*
LGBTQ+ Hotline	1-888-843-4564
National Suicide Prevention Hotline	1-800-273-TALK (8255)
Rainn Sexual Assault Hotline	1-800-656-HOPE
Substance Abuse/Mental Health Helpline	1-800-622-HELP
The Trevor Lifeline	866-488-7386
Trans Lifeline	1-877-565-8860

Online Articles & Social Media Resources

44 Mental Health Resources for Black People Trying to Survive in this Country	by Zahra Barnes
Depressed While Black	
Grief is a Direct Impact of Racism: Eight Ways to Support Yourself	by Roberta K. Timothy
How Racism, Trauma and Mental Health are Linked	by Christine Herman
I'm an Angry Black Man	by Jayson Kristopher
Melanated Social Work	
Mental Health Tips for African Americans to Heal After Collectively Witnessing an Injustice	by Brandon J. Johnson
Racism and Violence: How to Help Kids Handle the News	by Kenya Hameed & Jamie Howard
Representation Matters in Social Work: We Need More Black Therapists	by Relando Thompkins-Jones
Sharing Hope: Speaking with African Americans about Mental Health	
Treating Mental Health in the Black Community – Ask the Experts Webinar (YouTube)	
Uncovering the Trauma of Racism: New Tools for Clinicians	by Monnica T. Williams, Ph.D.

Organizations

Academics for Black Survival and Wellness	A Call To Men
African American Mental Health	All Us We Counseling, PLLC
A New Day MWC	Ayana Therapy
Better Day Better You Counseling & Consulting LLC	Black Boys OM, Inc.
Black Emotional and Mental Health Collective (BEAM)	
Black Executive Men	Black Men Cry Too
Black Men Feel	Black Men Heal
Black Men Meditate Too	Black Mental Health Advocac
Black Mental Health Alliance	Black Mental Health & Welln
Black Minds Collaborative	Black Minds Matter UK
Black Obsidian Men's Group	Black Students Talk
Black Therapists Rock	Boca Recovery Center
Brave Soul Collective	Breakout
Clinicians of Color	Consciously Coping
Coproduce Care	Darkness Rising Project
Dead The Silence	Eustress, Inc.
Golden Rhinos Mental Wellness Online Gathering	
Growing Boundlessly LLC	Healing While Black LLC
Henry Health	Huemen of Mental Health
Inclusive Therapists	InnoPsych – Therapy for BIPC
Intentional Therapy, Inc.	Just Heal Bro
Mastermind Connect	MEE Productions, Inc.

Melanin & Mental Health
Mental Health First Oakland
Mental Health Matters
My Brother's Keeper Cares
NAMI Maryland
National Organization for People of Color Against Suicide
NOBULLYMEINC
One Village Healing
Radical Therapy Center
Self-Care for Black Men
The Black Man, Inc.
The Campaign for Black Male Achievement
The Confess Project
The Healing Circle Foundation
The National Queer & Trans Therapists of Color Network
The OKRA Project
Therapy for Queer People of Color
The Sledge Group, Inc.
The Trevor Project

Mental Health America
Mental Health for Millennials
Men to Heal
Muslim Youth Helpline (MYH)

NYC Hip Hop Is Green
Queer BIPOC Mental Health Fund
RVA Mental Health Solidarity
The Aakoma Project

The Defensive Line

Therapy For Black Men
The Rise Center
The Triggered Project
Unlimited Potential

Podcasts

Aaron TLKS
Behavioral Health Today
Black Fathers, Now!
Detoxicity: By Men, About Men, For Everyone
Express Yourself Black Man
Living A Triggered Life
Mental Health Matters with Marty
Mental Hip Hop with Dr. S.
Mind of a Man Podcast
Rethinking Manhood
The Black Psychologist Podcast
The Fatherhood Village
The Male Perspective with Lana Reid
The WYATT! Podcast
#YouGoodMan? A Men's Wellness Podcast

ADHD Men's Support
Black Mental Health Podcast

Let's Talk Bruh
Melanated Mindfulness Mondays
Mental Health Mondays
Men Thrive
NO SKY Podcast
Tearapy Recovery Podcast
The Breakdown with Dr. Earl
The Lost and Found Podcast
The Man Initiative Podcast
Wellness House

Practitioners, Psychologists, Social Workers and Therapists

Saiyd Amir
Samuel Beavers, MSW
Nathaniel Currie
Marcus Gaddy
Wallace Ford
Justin Murray
Nafis Ricks
Christopher Scott, MSW, LSSW, CSWA
Dr. Jackey Smith, LCSW
Dr. Earl Turner
Antonio J. Wheeler, LCSW, CADC

Jeff Baker
Dr. Taisha Caldwell-Harvey
Kwame Dance
Vaughn Gay
Tyrone Melvin
Alphonso Nathan
Avery Rosser
Nigel Sealey
Marvin Tolliver
Shelton Watson, MSW

Support from Service Providers

www.alluswecounseling.com
www.amassi.com
www.anewdaymwc.org
www.arts-ave.org
www.betterdaybetteryoucc.com
www.bicyclehealth.com
www.blackexecutivemen.com
www.blackobsidianhealing.com
www.bocarecoverycenter.com
www.borislhensonfoundation.org
www.breakout.today
www.bushcounselingservices.com
www.cliniciansofcolor.org
www.consciouslycoping.com
www.coproducecare.com
www.demarquisclarke.com
www.drcandicenicole.com
www.drnortontherapy.com
www.drthema.com
www.freedomcommunityclinic.org
www.freeluxproject.org
www.getelevateapp.com
www.heardnotjudged.com
www.healhaus.com
www.heartsinmindcounseling.com
www.hiphopsocialworker.com

www.inclusivetherapists.com
www.integracionrelacional.com
www.intentionaltherapy.org
www.jardindogan.com
www.like-you.app
www.mastermindconnect.com
www.mentalhealthmarty.com
www.menthrive.com
www.mentoheal.com
www.mhnational.org
www.mytrucircle.com
www.nobullynme.org
www.psychhub.com
www.quadefyllc.net
www.reginaldahoward.com
www.startingpointecounseling.com
www.stevonlewis.com
www.suicidepreventionlifeline.org
www.tayeuhuru.com
www.tearapyrecovery.com
www.theesafeplace.org
www.theheartwerk.com
www.thementalhealthaccess.org
www.thementalhealthmatters.com
www.torrewashington.com
www.wabisabipsych.com

"*Cultural Silence and Wounded Souls: Black Men Speak about Mental Health*, edited by Mark Tuggle, unapologetically gives Black men the love and support we desperately need. This collection/gathering of Black men is sharing their innermost feelings, thoughts and experiences in an effort to heal themselves and all of us. I have been in therapy for nearly two decades. Like many Black men in America I the first decade in secret out of shame. This book affirms Black men. Their honest emotions, transparency and vulnerability is a gift to Black men. Mark offers Black men the grace of love, emotional support, freedom and encouragement we need."

– Andre' Robert Lee, Filmmaker.

"Mark Tuggle created space for Black men to be vulnerable, stand in their truth and further the path of individual healing and needed at the appointed time. Many spaces currently exist to heal and affirm the female psyche. *Cultural Silence and Wounded Souls: Black Men Speak about Mental Health* opens a door for Black men to acknowledge, accept, affirm and embrace their delicate souls. Society teaches us to fear Black men. Black men are socialized to hide their emotions. Black boys are expected to act like adults. No institution teaches us to accept and honor their humanity. As a result, unlike women, they suffer in silence. As the men in this book pour out their souls in its rawness it gives others permission to do the same. Cultural healing must start with individual healing. We cannot respect and honor each other until we first respect and honor self. All parts of the Black male psyche are welcome, needed and valued. A deep bow to Mark and these men for breaking their silence – not just for themselves but for the advancement of humanity."

– Debra Sledge, Founder Deborah4Greatness (The Home of Old Lady Magic) – Rites of Passage for Seasoned Sistas.

"*Cultural Silence and Wounded Souls: Black Men Speak about Mental Health* is the first book of its kind to bring together a collection of narratives centering Black men about their mental and emotional stability. The thoughts, feelings and sensations edited by Mark Tuggle are more common than most people realize. The fact people lack understanding of the mental state of Black men doesn't mean their humanity is less real or important. Mark honors a diversity of Black male experiences from the young to the elderly, across a variety of disciplines – and identities – to bring to light the raw, authentic, realities often shamed by mainstream sociopolitical and environmental contexts."   – *Bmen Foundation*

"I practiced medicine in New York for 40 years, primarily working with minority communities. One particularly challenging area was attempting to get Black men to accept psychotherapy or other behavioral health (BH) modalities. In my opinion, Black men are the toughest group of all to accept them. The stigma of having any type of BH interventions was almost as bad as being HIV-Positive. The 'I'm not crazy' reaction was pretty consistent. The idea that anxiety, depression or PTSD could destroy lives or the quality of life was very difficult to accept – it is seen as a weakness; you are less than a man. Some Black men told me 'I don't need that, they don't understand me.' Other Black men tried to snap out of it by using alcohol or drugs. The irony is they are one of the groups with the most emotional baggage and could probably benefit the most from BH services. I am grateful this compilation of essays is available, presented in a more humane and less threatening light, featuring other Black men speaking with deep logic, faith and intelligence on the subject."   – *Nereida Ferran-Hansard, MD*

"*Cultural Silence and Wounded Souls: Black Men Speak about Mental Health*, edited by Mark Tuggle, provides the insight and permission for Black Men to embrace and practice WHOLE HEALTH! For far too long, we have shied away and not talked about the importance of proactively practicing strong mental health. Mark has captured the essence of honoring mental health. This will go a long way in normalizing the conversation. I commend Mark's bravery, compassion and unapologetic approach to healing Black men. His research, care and knowledge can help thousands of Black youth understand 'It's OK to not be OK.' This will allow them to ask for help and save their lives. Sharing diverse, poignant and meaningful stories on mental health benefits the Black community. This is a must read for parents so they can equip Black youth with tools for understanding the value of whole health and connecting with each other."   – *Chris Thomas, CEO and Founder, The Defensive Line*

"As a Black professional who worked in the private health care sector as well as being an anti-racism campaigner for over three decades in the United Kingdom I am delighted such an important book has come along. The topic of BLACK MEN AND MENTAL HEALTH is a difficult and often taboo subject matter, due to the complex intersectionality of ethnicity, gender and well-trodden misconception that Black men are two legged beasts of burden incapable of feeling vulnerable or fragile.

This book explores the Black male psyche in a deeply personal way that astounds with poignancy and tugs at heart strings in equal measure. Regardless of who you are or where you're from you will undoubtedly benefit from the diverse perspectives in this thoroughly engaging book, filled with true life testimonies that are enlightening and educational. I nodded my head in agreement as each contributors' unique story began to resonate with my own experiences. I found myself somewhere between validation and acceptance.

This truly is an important book that has harnessed the power of those who have felt powerless and isolated and used it to empower and bring people together."

— Cliff Faulder, Founder and CEO, About Face Training and
About Face Publishing.

Made in the USA
Columbia, SC
23 May 2024

35597089R00083